"Please, Oh Please
Can We Get a Dog?"

"Please, Oh Please Can We Get a Dog?"

Parents' Guide to Dog Ownership

Cheryl Peterson

Copyright © 2005 by Wiley Publishing, Inc., Hoboken, New Jersey. All rights reserved.

Howell Book House
Published by Wiley Publishing, Inc., Hoboken, New Jersey

For general information on our other products and services or to obtain technical support please contact our Customer Care Department within the U.S. at (800) 762-2974, outside the U.S. at (317) 572-3993 or fax (317) 572-4002.

Wiley also publishes its books in a variety of electronic formats. Some content that appears in print may not be available in electronic books. For more information about Wiley products, please visit our web site at www.wiley.com.

Library of Congress Cataloging-in-Publication Data:

Peterson, Cheryl, date.
  Please oh please can we get a dog? : parents' guide to dog ownership / Cheryl Peterson.
    p. cm.
  Includes index.
  ISBN=10 0-7645-7297-0 (paper: alk. paper)
  ISBN=13 978-0-7645-7297-5 (paper: alk. paper)
  1. Dogs. 2. Children and animals. I. Title.
  SF426.P4465 2005
  636.7'0887—dc22
                                    2004024050

10 9 8 7 6 5 4 3 2 1

This book is printed on acid-free paper.

Book design by LeAndra Hosier
Cover design by Jose Almaguer
Book production by Wiley Publishing, Inc. Composition Services

Dedicated to Nordic's Hobo Zak, CD, loved and greatly missed.

Alone Again
By a dog who was once loved

I wish someone would tell me
What it is that I've done wrong.
Why I have to stay chained up
And left alone so long.
They seemed so glad to have me
When I came here as a pup.
There were so many things we'd do
While I was growing up.
They couldn't wait to train me
As their Companion and a Friend.
And told me how we'd always be
Together till the end.
The children said they'd feed me
And brush me every day.
They'd play with me and walk me
If only I could stay.
But now the children have no time,
They often say I shed.
They do not want me in the house
Not even to be fed.
The children never walk me
They always say "not now!"
I wish that I could please them
Won't someone tell me how?
I gave them all the love I had.
I wish they would explain
Why they said they wanted me
Then left me on a chain.

Contents

Acknowledgments

I would like to thank the following people for their support and help in putting this book together:

To my parents, Bette and the late Charles Peterson, who allowed me to gain experience in the sport of dogs and develop my love for animals at a young age. I would also like to thank my mother for her input and for taking over some of my chores so I could devote my time to this book and to meet my deadlines.

For editing and proofreading: Art Andres, Jill B. Day, Deborah Keas, and Dorothy Piper.

For professional assistance: Elizabeth Becker, M.S.; Clay Coady; Jason Randall, D.V.M.;. Joann Randall, D.V.M.; and Susan Kaneer Shirley, Ph.D.

For technical support: Karin Boullion.

For photographs: Alissa Behr/Pet Personalities, Animal Hospital of Woodstock, Karin Boullion, Tim Dyer, Cathy Gallagher, Garden Studio Inc., Tim Jorstad, Jan July, Marge Mehagian, Michael Shupp, and STM.

And finally, to my Howell Book House editor, Beth Adelman—thank you for finding a diamond in the "ruff."

Introduction

There is nothing more rewarding in life than a canine companion. No matter what happens, your four-legged friend is there to celebrate your good times and console you in your tough times, all with unconditional love and loyalty.

There will be plenty of days of running, jumping, and carefree playing, but there will also be the other side that is not so fun—the care, expense, and time you will spend with your dog nursing sickness and injury up to the time when you take the unselfish responsibility of letting go and saying a final good-bye.

Dog ownership is a wonderful adventure for parents and children. But first you must carefully examine your living situation and lifestyle to make sure a dog will fit in smoothly. You will be taking stewardship over a living being, who will depend on you for food, water, shelter, exercise, and health care. Unless you are sure it is the right thing at the right time for your family, you must give yourself permission to say "no" when your child asks for a dog.

In counseling families on dog ownership issues, I have found that many families entered into ownership with little or no education. Thus, for many, the end result was a failed human-dog relationship. There are many fine and honest breeders in all of the breeds that share the same desire: making the relationship between you and your dog a positive one. However, there are also "breeders" whose interest goes no further than whether your check cleared the bank. My concern is that you take the time to examine your options for dog ownership, and educate yourself about the breed and about reputable breeders. Helping you do that is the reason I wrote this book.

If you do decide to get a dog, there are more than 100 breeds to choose from. You'll need to carefully consider what you want in a dog. Learning about all the breeds to find the one for you can be a fun family activity.

You will be wise to educate yourself about your chosen breed. Don't buy the first puppy you see on impulse. The best place to find a healthy puppy is from a reputable breeder, and I will explain how to find breeders you can trust. Other good ideas are rescue groups, shelters, and reputable adoption programs. Once you have taken the time to read this book and explore some of the recommended resources, you will be able to find reputable breeders and organizations to get a healthy, happy dog.

Some of this material is a reality check for your life—a way to make you put your emotions on the back burner and look at your life more closely. In the end, doing your homework really does pay off.

Good luck with your new pal. I hope you run, jump, and play carefree for many years to come.

1

Panic!

Two of the most dreaded questions children ask their parents are:

- Where do babies come from?
- Please, oh please can we get a dog?

These questions seem to be inbred into all kids. And the usual parent response is—panic. Since you are reading this, it is safe to assume that the second question has cropped up at least once in your family's dinnertime discussions. If you have ever loved a dog, perhaps you understand your child's desire to own one. If you have not owned a dog or your view about dog ownership is generally negative, you will have to give the matter some objective thought before you can consider your child's request.

Owning a dog can be a wonderful experience that opens a child's mind to previously unknown pleasures—the pleasure of loving a living being; the pleasure of providing good care; the pleasure of seeing the world through a dog's eyes, which is a more down-to-earth, instinctual approach to life—all of which may help to ground your child in a world that is demanding a lot of him or her.

The right dog with the right child can be a wonderful partnership of fun, love, and understanding. That is the experience you can seek for your child.

The Magic of Children and Dogs

There is something magical about children and dogs. They have been depicted together for as long as artists have been painting portraits. Children are attracted to the unconditional love dogs give so freely. Many children delight in the way a dog can offer them complete attention. Parents, siblings, and teachers may be busy or distracted, but a dog gives the present of his presence in a way that is completely satisfactory and fulfilling. Dogs are willing to be companions and protectors of children. There are few sights as heartwarming as that of a child, sound asleep, with his arm around his dog. For outgoing, energetic children, a dog can provide a loyal playmate, one who will run with him and investigate the world. For lonely or book-loving children, a dog gives a reason to go out and exercise and possibly even make friends with someone else who has a dog. A dog will chase sticks or balls, or trot along at your feet, and can make the whole world fun.

Dogs can be the source of many lessons. From observing the behavior of his dog, a child can learn respect for others, acceptance, love, and empathy. Children will also learn that the world is not always fair, and sometimes it is necessary to go home and lick your wounds. Dogs live only in the present, not in memories from the past or anticipation of the future. So no matter what happens to them, as soon as they regain their equilibrium dogs are back to being happy, tail-wagging creatures, looking for fun or a pat on the head. Dogs naturally possess a positive outlook on life, which has proven to be a great help to children who feel sad or depressed.

In taking care of their dogs, children can learn responsibility, commitment, and how to handle a position of authority in a loving way. Kids who have dogs are usually more compassionate and more gentle than kids without them.

Janet Willmann, an elementary schoolteacher, says, "I know for a fact that animals develop responsibility in a child. I often bring my Whippet, Indy, to school. It amazes me to see how the presence of the dog settles the kids. They are more kind and gentle to each other when he is around. A dog is a great friend to a child. He can be a good listener as well as a great playmate."

Unconditional Love

"Growing up with a dog teaches kids unconditional love," says dog breeder Wendy Jones. "It teaches them respect. I think growing up with a dog can also help kids be more social. I grew up with dogs, but my husband didn't. It took meeting mine and then having one of his own to break through a twenty-year fear of dogs, and now he is the happiest dog person I've ever seen. If only he'd been more exposed to dogs when he was younger, he would have learned more about the loving side of himself. It breaks my heart to see children run or shriek in fear of a strange dog because they've never had the delight of owning one, and their parents have never taken the time to teach them to love animals."

Dog owner Renée Clayton says, "I believe I am a better person *because* I was raised with dogs. I learned how to be caring, patient, and responsible. I feel it is a loss to a child *not* to have a pet as a companion. Loving a dog teaches a child how to love someone other than themselves. I would also like to believe I am smarter, because I had to out-think the dogs in my life!"

Another dog owner, Jennifer Penman, says, "Like me, owning a dog could help a nine or ten-year old overcome shyness. Taking a dog to obedience classes gets you out of your shell. You have to become a leader of your little pack of two. I became so much more confident after I got my dog. He looked up to me, and I felt that I had to show him that everything was all right. And while I was acting that way, it became easier for me to talk to other kids."

Life is constantly changing, and today we live in a world where some families have become "decentralized." The family unit is not quite as interconnected as it once was. Dual-income families are the standard. This places more stress on parents, who often worry about providing enough love, time, guidance, and support to their kids. Although the majority of parents actually manage quite well, the reality is that children, who require and thrive on unconditional love, get less of it than they did twenty years ago.

Please, oh please can I have this puppy?

Those families who are able to participate together in the care and raising of a dog introduce a heightened feeling of love in their homes that children benefit from immensely. Marketing expert Chuck Carroll says, "A kid today, due to no fault of his parents, goes through childhood with a little bit less than we had, in terms of loving connections. A dog can take up the slack by leaving important, positive, emotional impressions at a time and in a world where diminished intimacy can be a child's greatest loss."

As an added benefit, recent medical studies suggest that children who grow up in a home with animals have fewer allergies as adults. The theory so far is that regular exposure to the allergens associated with pets stimulates the immune system and heads off allergic reactions later in life.

The Commitment of Dogs

As wonderful as dogs are, they are a family responsibility—one that needs to be shared, rather than foisted upon a child. Many families already manage too much responsibility, and dogs probably should not be added to the list. Owning a dog means having stewardship of a living being, one who is totally dependent on you to provide for his care. It is not the same as buying a car. You cannot leave it to rust in the yard and then trade it in for a new model when some of the luster has worn off.

Many people have fond memories of childhood. They forget that usually mom was home all the time and there were fewer activities for kids after school. They get a puppy, don't train him, he becomes a bother, and they all soon tire of the pup. He then ends up at the local shelter.

Ten Things about Kids and Dogs

These reasons a child benefits from having a dog come from Donna Rotman Miner in Coventry, Connecticut.

1. Kids learn about unconditional love.
2. Kids learn patience.
3. Kids learn to value life.
4. Dogs help kids understand the life cycle, including death.
5. Dogs help kids develop empathy for another being.
6. Kids learn how to communicate with another being in a way that does not include force.
7. Young children who have pets are less likely to have asthma and allergies.
8. A dog can help a child who suffers from depression.
9. A dog is always a shoulder to cry on and someone to love.
10. A dog is a good way to get rid of your peas when your parents aren't looking.

During the discussion about getting a dog, the whole family needs to be aware that together you are making a commitment that will last for more than a decade. As in any relationship, a commitment needs to be complete and ongoing. Parents must work with their children on responsibility issues, but they also must be realistic. Children's chores should be divided and age appropriate. It is unfair to expect a five-year-old child to clean up the yard, but it is not unreasonable to expect a nine-year-old to do so. Even with cooperative kids, some chores will be the parents' responsibility. So before you do anything else, ask yourself this question: Am I willing to take over the day-to-day chores when the novelty of the puppy wears off? This question is especially for you, mom, because unfair as it is, the responsibilities of dog care often fall disproportionally onto you.

Kids—even the best kids—need help with the dog's feeding, walking, bathing, and vet appointments. The parents will have to pitch in on these jobs to some extent, no matter how much the kids claim otherwise. You cannot let the kids neglect the dog just to teach them a lesson about responsibility, because this is unfair to your dog.

Fran Chaput Waksler, a professor of sociology at Wheelock College in Boston who studies children's perspectives, says, "Some children simply want a dog, some even want one desperately. That strikes me as an excellent reason for them to have one. But one flaw I see in advice often given about children and dogs is that the child should be responsible for the dog. I strongly disagree. I think the responsibility is ultimately the adult's, and it is naive to think otherwise. Recognizing this from the outset will avoid problems for the adult, the child, and the dog. Dogs are not teaching tools; they are family members."

She recalls, "I was given a dog at age five, not long after my father died. It was the best gift in the world. As I look back, I realize that as a child I had no responsibility for the dog; others fed him and let him out, and my job was to love him. As I got older, I took on more of the care just because it seemed the right thing to do for *my* dog."

These Viszla puppies will be around for more than a decade and will need consistent love and care.

Dogs are very time-consuming. Adding a dog is in many ways like adding another child to your family. He is like a child who stops growing mentally at the human equivalent of four years old, yet needs continual care for his entire lifetime—which may be twelve years or more. A dog cannot be treated like a pair of shoes, passing him on when he no longer suits you. He is an animal with feelings and attachments. It's not fair to the dog, and it most definitely teaches your kids the wrong lesson about commitment, love, and respect for other living things.

Help for Geeks and Nerds

"Speaking from experience, having a dog as a kid was one of the best things that ever happened to me," says experienced Whippet breeder Annie Whitney. "At age eight I got my first Whippet, but I was too young to take care of it. Our family got a second Whippet two years later. That second Whippet was mine. No matter what his papers may have said, he was my best friend.

"Throughout junior high and high school, I was your typical nerd/geek/loner, so I had few friends to hang out with. But I always had my dog. I could have had the worst day, but I always counted on Walter to be there for me. I would talk to him and tell him all that was going on—stuff no kid would say to their parents. And without a ton of friends, having the dog there was a big stress reliever. Those school years can be the worst for any kid."

"When selling a dog to someone with kids, I make sure the parents want the dog, too, and don't just think they are getting a living toy," says Annie Whitney, a Whippet breeder.

If both parents are not in agreement about a dog, the chance of having a successful relationship is jeopardized. You would be well advised to wait until all family members are ready for a dog.

The Research

When you decide to go ahead with dog ownership, you will also need to explore which breed and which dog is right for you. A dog is not a surprise gift. As most breeders will tell you, picking out the right dog is a very personal matter. The potential owner of the dog has to make sure that, yes, this is the right dog for me. You don't want to bring home a surprise Chihuahua, only to learn that your child's heart was set on a German Shepherd.

Through my years of rescue work, it has become apparent that people jump into dog ownership with too little thought and preparation. In the

As Mel and Becka prove, the right dog can be a perfect companion for every member of the family.

end, the family is unhappy and the dog is turned over to the nearby shelter in search of a new home. Unfortunately, for many dogs life ends there.

With proper education and preparation, the stresses and concerns of buying a dog can be greatly reduced. To assist you on the road to dog ownership, I will address the most frequently asked questions and attempt to provide answers. This book will introduce issues that people seldom think about when they get a family pet. Hopefully, you will gain insight and education to use in your decision-making process.

2

Are You Ready for a Dog?

You must put a great deal of thought into analyzing your lifestyle to see what kind of dog will complement it. You'll need to realistically examine your home life, work, family, economics, leisure activities, travel, and health-related problems. You must accurately and honestly assess your situation, so that you can avoid disappointment for both you and your family. Knowing your family's limitations will greatly increase your chances of having a successful relationship with your dog. You will be able to find the dog who best fits into your family. You may want a Golden Retriever, for example, but find out, once you examine your current lifestyle, that a Boston Terrier better suits your needs.

Take the time to really think about these questions, talk about them with the other members of your family, and write down the answers. In chapter 4 I'll give you a list of questions to consider about the dog breeds you are interested in. Write down your answers to those questions as well. Then compare your two lists. This is the best way to find a dog who will fit in with your family's lifestyle.

How Long Are You Gone Each Day?

Your personal and family schedule should weigh in very heavily in your decision to get a dog. For instance, if both parents work, how many hours will your dog be left alone? It is just a fact of life that a puppy and an older dog cannot be expected to hold their bladder and bowels all day long. If there is no one to take the puppy out every four or five hours, when you get home you will be greeted by an exuberant, dirty puppy who will also need to be bathed, have his crate cleaned, and be fed and walked. When you have a chance to sit down, the little guy will want to play and eventually have to go out again. So say good-bye to your favorite television shows until your puppy gets older. Plus, you may have a dog who is more difficult to housetrain.

There are ways you can avoid this scenario, but some of them depend on your budget. You can hire a dog walker who will come in and walk, play with, and feed your dog during your absence. The number of walks your dog needs in a day depends not only on your budget, but also on the age of your dog and the distance you work from home. For an adult dog whose owners live within thirty to forty-five minutes from work, a midday walk should suffice, but with young puppies or older dogs with health concerns, two walks during the day may be required.

Some dog walkers offer time-saving services, such as taking your dog to the groomer and the veterinarian. Of course, extra services cost more, but the time saved may be worth it to you. What is nice about using a dog walker is that your dog stays in his familiar home surroundings and has less of a chance of picking up an illness or parasite from other dogs.

Another option is doggie daycare. As with child care, you drop your dog off in the morning and pick him up in the evening. At these facilities your dog is played with, fed, and socialized with other dogs. You should check to see if the facility is licensed to board dogs overnight should the need arise, particularly if you sometimes have to work late or if your job includes last-minute business trips.

If you feel uncomfortable about strangers coming into your home, or are not keen on crating your dog all day, or your schedule makes it difficult to work around daycare center hours, there is another alternative: build a kennel for the dog. Kennels can be built inside the house in a basement or laundry room or any other place with a floor that's easy to keep clean. It is especially nice to have a drain nearby for the ease of cleaning. Kennels can also be built outside and attached to the garage or to a freestanding doghouse, but they must offer your dog shelter from temperature extremes and bad weather. The materials you need can be picked up at home centers and can be configured into a variety of sizes and styles as elaborate as you design the kennel to be.

A dog can be a friend for life. This is Chase Williams and her Whippet, Maya.

When the outdoor temperatures go from one extreme to another, dogs suffer. With indoor kennels, the temperature can be regulated so that weather conditions are not a concern. Northern breeds love cold weather, but if you choose a shorthaired dog, you will have one unhappy Doberman Pinscher shivering and hopping from foot to foot to keep warm.

Just remember, though, that a dog cannot spend the majority of each day alone in a kennel. Dogs are pack animals, and they get bored and lonely by themselves. If you don't have time to spend with your dog every day, this may not be the right time to get a dog.

Does Your Job Require You to Travel?

Business travel can often interfere with dog ownership. If you need to travel frequently and you are the only adult caretaker for the dog, you may have a difficult time finding someone to watch the dog in your absence, unless you are lucky enough to have a generous neighbor or relative who will volunteer. Even volunteers cannot be counted on in every circumstance. With that in mind, you may need to investigate boarding facilities in your area.

Check out their rates, facilities, and services available to you and your dog. Boarding a dog can become quite expensive. In addition, you need to find out how much lead time the facility needs to save a space for your dog—especially near the holidays, when some kennels are booked up to three months in advance.

Your dog walker or a licensed pet sitter may be able to care for your dog while you're gone, but again, you need to give them lead time so that they can fit you into their schedule. You need to plan ahead as much as possible to make appropriate care arrangements. If your business requires frequent trips on short notice, you might do better to put off dog ownership.

Do You Travel Frequently for Pleasure?

Think about your family vacations. If you fly across the country or to another continent for a vacation every year, what will you do with your dog? If you like to take off every weekend in the winter to ski, or in the summer to go to the beach, can the dog come with you? If not, who will look after him?

Recently, I read a question in an advice column from a woman who invited a family friend to visit her for the holiday. She requested the friend not bring his dog. Well, to her amazement, when she went to answer the door, the man and his dog were standing at the door. She said the four days were an absolute nightmare for her family, because her children suffered from allergies and were not accustomed to having an animal in the house. The kids were crabby because they didn't feel well and were not prepared to protect themselves from a rambunctious dog who jumped up on them and knocked them over. Even two months later, her youngest daughter was still afraid of dogs. Because of the allergies in the family, the rooms needed extensive cleaning to remove dog hair and dander after the guest left.

This friend is not going to get an invitation back any time soon! Remember that even though you think your dog is the best dog in the world, others may not see it that way.

If it is necessary to travel with your dog, you must ask your hosts *in advance* if they mind having a canine guest. If they request no dog, you must respect their wishes. One solution is to kennel the dog at a facility near where you are visiting, so you can see him every day. You can ask your host to help you find nearby kennels to contact.

Whether you board the dog back home or in your destination city, it is important to keep the dog's vaccinations up to date. Every boarding kennel will ask for a veterinarian's health certificate or proof of vaccination before boarding your dog. The more you board your dog, however, the more vet bills you are likely to incur, since the dog is more likely to pick up illnesses and parasites at even the cleanest kennels.

Is Your Living Space Suitable for the Dog You Want?

Before you get a dog, take a close look at your living space to make sure it can accommodate the size and energy level of the dog you want. Of course, the best situation is a single-family home with a fenced-in yard, but while that's an advantage, it's not a requirement. A fenced-in yard enables you to stay warm and dry in inclement weather while the dog goes out and does his business. Having your own yard gives you a handy place to play with your dog, too. Although the yard may be fenced, it may need some work before it is ready for a dog; dogs are masters at digging under and jumping over fences.

Many dogs do well in an apartment, provided you take the dog out several times a day (four is usually about right) and provide adequate exercise. While large breeds will become accustomed to apartment living, it is vital from a health standpoint that they get out several times a week for vigorous exercise. Toy breeds, for the most part, can get a good amount of exercise from running around the apartment, but exercise outside is necessary for them, too.

Taking your dog to an appropriate, fenced-in place for exercise can be time consuming, and the nearest area where it is legal to let your dog off leash may not be very near your apartment. You must provide this exercise throughout the dog's life and in all kinds of weather, so decide

Notre Dane's Andre, a Great Dane, getting his exercise with owner Patti Runchey.

whether you have the time to devote to exercising your dog, especially if you want a large breed who is active. Dogs are like kids: If they cannot get out to play to rid themselves of their pent-up energy, they can be *very* difficult (and very unhappy) to live with.

What floor do you live on? Owning a dog and living on the second floor of an apartment complex or living on the forty-second floor of a city high-rise are two very different things, especially with a puppy. Living on the forty-second floor with a puppy means by the time you get to the first floor to take the puppy out to potty and get back up to the forty-second floor, it is time to go out again! Some people now litter train their small dogs, but I wouldn't suggest this practice for a Great Dane!

Think, too, about how you keep your house. Is it furnished with valuable antiques and expensive carpets? It's inevitable that a new puppy will have accidents on the floor and chew on your chair legs, and even an adult dog will get hair all over everything. If you can't stand the thought of anything being out of place or fuzzy or damaged in your home, perhaps a dog is not for you.

What Will Your Landlord Say?

Will your lease or co-op agreement allow you to have a pet? Many dogs are given up to rescue groups and shelters because their owner forgot to read the lease. Some landlords will charge an extra monthly fee or a large deposit up front that goes toward repairing any damage caused by the dog. Sometimes, the money is refundable if there is no damage. Check your lease to see if it has a provision like this. Co-ops, condos, and even planned communities may also have no-pets provisions or clauses that limit the size or number of dogs you can have.

One woman I know got a small dog even though she knew she had a no-dogs lease. She covered the dog up with a blanket whenever she took him out and made sure she carried him far away from the building before putting him down. She got away with this for several months, until the landlord had to go into her apartment to make an emergency repair. Oops! The landlord gave her a choice of who would leave: the dog, her, or both. By this time she was very attached to the dog and did not want to give him up, but she couldn't find a similar apartment in her price range. Bottom line: *read your lease.*

Sometimes, leases say nothing either way about pets. However, talk with the landlord first. You might offer to pay a "pet charge" up front or each month. One important factor to keep in mind in any rental situation is *you must please your landlord and neighbors to maintain your privilege of dog ownership,* even in a dog-friendly building. If there are complaints about noise, smell, and untidiness on the grounds, you may be asked to either leave or get rid of your pet.

If you are planning to relocate any time soon, remember that finding a pet-friendly building is not easy. You might find it wiser to put off getting a dog until you are sure your new job will work out and you have found appropriate living arrangements.

A litter of Vizsla puppies exploring their surroundings.

Will Your Family's Leisure Activities Accommodate Your Dog?

What are your hobbies? We all enjoy some activities where dogs are not welcomed, such as going to the movies, but what other activities do you and your family enjoy that can include the family dog? Perhaps you enjoy walking, jogging, camping, or fishing, all of which your dog can participate in with you. Maybe your kids regularly spend an hour or more each day playing with their friends in the yard.

Dogs are pack animals and enjoy being with you. By participating in family activities, your dog will be able to get the exercise he needs and work on his social skills during his various interactions with people and other dogs.

Although walking is a good way to spend time with your pet, for many breeds it provides as much exercise as pushing the button on the TV remote control—unless you are prepared to go for a very *long* walk every single day. A small dog such as a Basenji will get good exercise from a three-mile walk three times a week. A Border Collie may need a three-mile jog every day.

Think about how much exercise you can provide for a dog, then find out how much exercise the breed you want should get (see chapter 7). You may have to pick another breed if your first choice turns out to be more than your family can handle. You may also have to pick another breed if you all want a Bulldog but you like to go on long mountain hikes. Not every dog can keep up with every type of activity. You'll really need to find a dog whose activity level matches your own.

If your family is into outdoor activities, choose a breed that can enjoy those activities with you.

How Old Are Your Children?

This question has to be one of the most important you need to consider. We all think our children are angels but, in reality, they can sometimes show the little devil in them. Children under the

Will He Bite Again?

One evening, I received a call from a desperate family. Their dog had bitten their fifteen-year-old son. When I asked what caused the dog to bite, the mother replied that it was the teen's fault. She had repeatedly told her son not to jump on the dog when the dog was sleeping. On this particular evening, the dog was sleeping peacefully, curled up on the end of the couch. The teenager charged in and pounced on him. The startled dog responded with a bite that required stitches to the boy's face.

This was the only time in all my years of doing rescue work that a parent actually blamed her child for a bite from the family dog. The mother worried that her son's action might result in a dog who would bite again. She took my suggestion to work with an animal behavior specialist. The last time I spoke with the family, everything was going smoothly and the dog and teen were best friends again.

age of seven have a tendency to pull ears, tails, and fur, and to hit dogs, not understanding that their actions hurt the animal. The result may be that the child is snapped at or bitten in self-defense. The family blames the dog and takes him to the shelter. There is generally only one end for a dog who has bitten a child: he is destroyed. So you can see that your decision affects more lives than you realize.

When something is bothering him, a dog will generally try to get away from the situation. If he can't, he may bark or growl his warning, and if the confrontation continues, he may snap or bite. But who is really at fault? Young children often do not realize the consequences of their actions. The dog is defending himself, which is only natural. Most of the blame for these attacks should be placed on the parents for their lack of supervision.

The rule with any animal, whether it is a dog, cat, bird, or reptile, is *never leave your child unsupervised with the family pet.* Even the few minutes it takes to answer the telephone can be too long. *Avoid the problem by thinking wisely.*

Dachshunds Muffy and McDuff, owned by Emma and Sarah Sakson.

Only you can evaluate your child's level of maturity. I have seen four-year-old children who are very well behaved and nine year olds who constantly defy their parents. The best way to gauge if your children are truly ready for a pet is easy: if you have to keep repeating and reminding them not to do something, then they are not ready for a dog. Ignoring these warning signs can have disastrous results.

Your best bet is to start working on responsibility issues with your children to prepare them for a future pet. By setting goals for your child, she knows she can work toward getting a dog based upon her accomplishments. Only when you believe your child understands how to behave with an animal and what her responsibility will be, should you bring a pet into the family.

What Health Problems Run in Your Family?

Many people get a dog without thinking there might be health repercussions. The latest medical research suggests that children who live with a dog actually have fewer allergies and asthma as they grow up. The early exposure to a dog, and the plant material on his coat, may actually "tune up" their immune systems so they can deal with such stresses later.

However, it is possible that having an animal in the house can exacerbate existing allergies and asthma. Discuss any concerns you have with your doctor, and remember that an allergy does not mean you cannot have a dog. There may be treatment options available to you, perhaps as simple as taking allergy medication. More serious cases may require injections every month.

If a member of your family has allergy problems, certain breeds will be eliminated during your research. However, you should still be able to find a few breeds that meet your criteria. The lower maintenance breeds, such as the single-coated, short-coated varieties, often work out well since they shed very little. When dirty, they can be quickly wiped off and dried in a matter of minutes. Certain dogs with a double coat, such as Poodles, also tend to be easier on allergy sufferers. I know many people with allergies who, with a little extra effort in dusting, vacuuming, and doing laundry, enjoy their family dog with no ill effects.

Can You Afford to Keep a Dog?

Puppies aren't cheap. Depending on your puppy's pedigree and the breed's popularity, you can expect to spend anywhere from $300 to $2,000 for your dog. Even if you can easily afford the initial purchase price of a puppy, don't overlook the other expenses you will incur just to bring the puppy home. You can expect to spend several hundred dollars on the initial vet exam, shots, licenses, food, crate, and toys. Your dog will also need yearly veterinarian visits. Even if he has no health crises during the year, he still needs a heartworm test, heartworm medications, vaccines, and a general check-up.

As you can see from the chart on p. 22, it's expensive to own a dog. If you are not prepared, the cost and responsibility can sometimes be overwhelming. If you are on a very limited budget, you may want to investigate working with a breed rescue organization or go to recommended shelters and other animal welfare agencies for a mixed-breed dog. That will help you with the initial purchase price, but you still must be prepared to give your dog good food and good veterinary care for the rest of his life. Dogs deserve no less.

Expense	One-Time	Yearly
Price of dog	$700*	—
Vet visits	$70	$380†
License	—	$20
Food	$10–20	$420‡
Crate	$100	—
Toys/shampoo	$20	$50
Grooming (six times a year)	—	$300
Training	$250	—
Total	$1,160	$1,170§

* Less for adopting through a shelter or rescue organization; more for many breeds.
† Includes heartworm test, preventive medication, and annual check-up but not major medical problems.
‡ Based on forty pounds per month of dry dog food at $35 per bag (it will be less for little dogs).
§ Does not include boarding fees, dog walkers, or doggy daycare.

Is Your Marriage Healthy?

This may seem like an overly personal question, but it's one you need to ask yourself. A dog adds stress through demands for attention, food, and exercise. If you and your spouse are in counseling, you should forego pet ownership until your situation is more stable. If you and your spouse decide to part company, a new dog just makes things even more complicated. Many times, the dog turns out being the biggest loser.

Are You Planning to Add to Your Family?

If you and your spouse are planning to have a child, you might be wise to put off getting a dog until the child is at least seven years old. At that age, most children can understand basic rules concerning a dog, such as not pulling his ears or tail. Both the puppy and the baby require a major time commitment, and if time is at a premium, the dog loses out. A dog needs time to adjust to his new family and training to develop his social skills.

If you have no plans for children now but think you might want a child later on, choose a dog with small children in mind. An older, less active dog or breed may be your best bet, because young puppies often push children into an end table or accidentally knock them down, causing injury. It does not make for a positive experience for anyone in the household. An adult dog is more settled and tends to get less excited. A medium dog, perhaps the size of a Brittany, Sheltie, or Keeshond, may be best suited for your family.

Are You a Single Parent?

Single parents with small children may find that they need to rely on extended family or friends to help out. The work of training and socializing a dog is added to the chores of taking their children to softball practice or piano lessons. If in doubt, you may want to wait until your children are mature enough to help out before bringing a dog into the family.

Families should try to include the family pet as much as possible in their activities, whether it is a day at the park, a picnic, or a visit to the grandparents' home. Children need to be taught that even if they are visiting family friends, they must walk and clean up after their dog. These are the duties of a responsible dog owner. You may be amazed at how well your children do, once they understand the importance of their responsibilities. Make them aware of how their responsibilities affect not only the dog, but other people around them as well.

The Major Rule of Commitment

If you have any doubts at all about your ability to meet the commitments required in taking care of a dog—wait! The time is not right. Once you own a dog, his life is in your hands and he depends on you to provide food, shelter, medical care, and companionship for him. Make sure you're ready.

Good friends: Cassi and her Labrador Retriever, Amber.

3

Saying No to Your Child

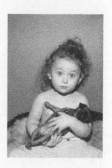

Saying no to a child can be very difficult, and no parent likes to do it. Parents usually use two different types of "no." One is, "No, and no is final," which means, "Not ever." Then there is, "No, not now," which means, "Maybe later." It is up to you to help your child understand the difference.

When "No" Means No

"No, and no is final" may be your answer for reasons that are permanently beyond your control. It may be impossible to bring an animal into the home because a family member suffers from allergies or other health conditions—in other words, something that does not change over time. Susan Kaneer Shirley, Ph.D., a licensed clinical professional counselor, has worked with parents and children on the issues involved in pet ownership. Shirley encourages parents in this situation to be completely honest with their child and to acknowledge his feelings.

"When a child asks for a pet, parents need to ask themselves why," says Shirley. "Is it an impulsive request because a friend just got a dog, or there was a cute dog on television or is it a genuine request? If it is a genuine request, most often it is because of the child's need for companionship, for something alive he can love and be loved by."

She advises, "Reason with the child using language such as, 'I am really sorry we cannot have a dog because I know how much you want one. But do you remember how sick your brother got after he petted Rex? It is not your brother's fault or Rex's fault. It is because your brother has a bad allergy to dog dander. It makes him sad, too.' This will help the child understand that this denial is not intended to punish him or deny him the companionship he is seeking, but rather is because someone gets sick and that, and only that, is the reason the family cannot have a dog."

Sociologist Fran Waksler of Cambridge, Massachusetts, suggests that parents be honest with themselves about why they are saying no. Her research has shown that children are especially troubled by lies. For example, one child was told the answer was "no" because her father had an allergy to dogs. She learned later that he had no such allergy, and she was understandably angry.

Waksler suggests that sometimes parents lie to conceal reasons that might put them in a bad light. They might tell the child, "No, because dogs are dirty," or "No, because dogs are too much work." These reasons are presented as "true" when in fact they are relative. Children see through these excuses, and may feel angry and cheated.

Waksler says, "The children who seem to be in the worst position are those who passionately want a dog and are denied one. They may well hold it against their parents for a long time, even if they never overtly show their distress."

When "No" Means Later

The other "no" is "No, not now," which can be difficult to explain. Be honest in your explanation. Acknowledge your child's disappointment. If the problem is that the family is living someplace where dogs are not allowed, that situation may change if the family moves. Or if the child lacks the emotional maturity to care for a dog, that situation may change when the child matures.

"How the child interacts with other children and plays with his toys are good indicators of how ready he is for the responsibility of a pet. If the child pushes or hits other children or acts roughly with toys, he will need to learn better social skills before he can be trusted with a pet. Transferred to a dog, such behavior could create a dangerous situation," Shirley says.

Children Remember These Things

"I had wanted a dog for as long as I could remember. When I was nine, I asked my parents why I couldn't have one. They told me that I had to first show them that I was responsible enough for a dog. That summer I got a paper route to show them how responsible I could be. I kept the stupid thing for a year, then asked again for a dog. They still said no, only this time they thought up another excuse. I was so mad at them that I quit the paper route and didn't talk to them unless I absolutely needed to for a long time."

—From Frances Chaput Waksler's *The Little Trials of Childhood and Children's Strategies for Dealing with Them* (London: Falmer Press, 1996)

Don't get involved in negotiations for a dog that place the burden of care entirely on the child. That's an unreasonable expectation. You can ask a child to take on some of the dog's care, but not all of it. How old the child is will determine what expectations you should have. For example, a six-year-old cannot do all the feeding, walking, and cleaning up after a dog. With a child under eleven, you cannot expect the child to do much more than one small chore for the animal. However, children learn responsibility by doing small repetitive chores. Give the child a responsibility he can handle, such as making sure the dog's water dish is always full. When the child is successful with this task, build on it by adding another. The important point is to protect the child (and the dog) from failing in his relationship with the dog, Shirley adds.

Learning to help takes time—even with older children. If the child genuinely is a "dog person," he may figure out in time, even without nagging, that dog care is simply a part of having a dog. In my experience, this learning may take as long as a year and then "magically" happen. I'd be inclined to recommend that adults plan on doing all the work of dog care at first, and expect that, in time, they can give up some or all of that care.

Shirley mentioned that one of her clients had a problem with her son; he constantly forgot to feed his dog. After several reminders, the mother took action. She decided that the next time her son forgot to feed his dog, he would miss his own dinner. When her son asked for dinner, his mother explained, "You are dependent on me for food, and Rex is dependent on you. Since you forgot to feed Rex, he is hungry. I want you to know how Rex feels." This proved to be an effective strategy for this family.

If the child is young, perhaps another type of pet who requires less care would be a better way to proceed, such as a goldfish, a turtle, or a hamster. These pets have fewer needs than a dog and are easier for your child to care for, of course under your supervision. When he can successfully handle the needs of a small pet, he may be ready to move up to a dog—again, with your help.

Is a Compromise Possible?

Sometimes, adults say no for selfish reasons and then try to pass off their reasons as either "right" or "for the good of the child"—both of which are excuses most children will see through. Ask yourself: Why am I saying no and am I being honest and fair in saying it? Is "no" negotiable or not? Can a resolution be found? Some parents wouldn't mind getting a dog but see obstacles, while others have decided they simply won't get a dog and are trying to get the child to accept that fact without the adult looking bad.

"Legitimate" reasons may be less straightforward than they appear. It may be useful to ask: If this problem was being faced by an adult, how might it be resolved? If an adult lived in an apartment that does not allow pets and really wanted one, they would move. If an adult had an allergy, they would get a Miniature Schnauzer, a Poodle, or some other breed that does not put so much stress on allergy sufferers. If the problem was that the family went sailing every weekend, the adult might get a Schipperke, since they were bred as barge dogs, or check with people who sail and have their dogs onboard.

Asking the child to do the research into what breed of dog might resolve the problem would serve as a measure of the child's commitment. But if you do set this up as a test, you must follow through with the child, or he may come to view you as untrustworthy.

Nicholas Shupp and his Vizsla, Kaiser.

If getting a dog is absolutely impossible, try finding other avenues for your child to have contact with animals. Explain the problem to a dog-owning neighbor and ask if your child could take their dog for a walk after school. This might help fill your child's need for contact with an animal and might even help them learn new responsibilities. Older children may be able to work at a veterinarian's office, the local shelter, or set up a pet sitting service. This option might involve adults in driving children to and fro, but no more than they would for soccer games or dance lessons. I knew an eight year old who volunteered at Greyhound Friends. This was not "baby" work—she walked dogs, cleaned kennels, and even sat at the information table at public events.

There are few relationships a child can have that are as rewarding as a relationship with a dog. Teaching a child the skills to care for him is a gift that will last a lifetime.

4

What Type of Dog Should You Get?

By now you know that it is vital to do your research before you get a dog, so that you can make an informed decision. A dog is a commitment you will have for a very long time, and this is not a choice to be made lightly or on a whim. Hopefully, you have honestly evaluated your family and lifestyle, as I described in chapter 2. In this chapter, I'll help you get a better idea of what type of dog will best fit in with your family. Characteristics you should consider include the type of coat, appearance, the height and weight of the dog at maturity, activity level, and temperament.

As you compare your list of family characteristics and canine characteristics, a profile should emerge of the right dog for you. You'll have to do some research to find out what breeds fit that profile. There may be several breeds in the running for your family dog, and you must turn your efforts to educating yourself about the breeds that interest you. I'll give you some tips on how to do that. Thinking about the questions in this chapter will help you narrow down your choices.

Thinking about Breeds

Today there are 156 breeds and varieties recognized by the American Kennel Club (AKC). (Varieties are variations of a breed that are shown separately, such as the Poodle, which comes in Standard, Miniature, and Toy. All are the same breed, but they do not compete against one another in the breed ring.) These breeds are organized into seven groups: Sporting, Hound, Working, Terrier, Toy, Non-Sporting, and Herding.

The Sporting Group contains dogs that have been used by humans for hunting game birds. The breeds are broken down to pointers, retrievers, and flushers (spaniels). The pointing breeds, such as Weimaraners and German Shorthaired Pointers, locate the birds on land and "point" out their location to the hunter, then retrieve the downed birds on land or water. The retrieving dogs, such as Labrador Retrievers and Flat-Coated Retrievers, are used mostly to retrieve water fowl in a variety of weather conditions. The flushers, such as English Springer Spaniels, locate the game and drive it into the air.

The Hound Group contains primarily two different types of hounds: sighthounds and scenthounds. Sighthounds are those who follow their prey by sight, such as Greyhounds, Whippets, and Afghan Hounds. They are lean and fast, and love to run. Scenthounds use the power of their nose to find their prey. They have long, hanging ears that help direct scent to their sensitive noses, and often walk with their head held low to the ground. These breeds include Beagles, Basset Hounds, and Bloodhounds.

Breeds in the Working Group perform duties of guarding, pulling, rescue work. They tend to be large and sturdy. The Doberman Pinscher, Newfoundland, and St. Bernard are examples of breeds in this group.

Non-Sporting dogs come in a wide array of appearances and personalities. The name Non-Sporting hails from the earliest days of dog shows, when there were only two groups, Sporting and Non-Sporting. Dogs in this group include the Dalmatian, Bulldog, and Poodle. While these dogs are not companions for hunters, many of the Non-Sporting breeds originally had a job to do. Dalmatians were bred to travel with horse-drawn coaches and protect them. Bulldogs were bred for fighting—a sport that has long been outlawed. And the well-known Poodle, with his strange hairdo, actually hunted with his master in old Europe. The pompoms and fluffy chest ruff he wears today originally had the purpose of keeping those parts of his body warm, yet allowing him enough free movement to swim out through cold water to retrieve a bird.

The Terrier Group's service to humans involves hunting and killing rodents, and includes breeds such as the Parson Russell Terrier (formerly known as the Jack Russell Terrier), Scottish Terrier, and Miniature Schnauzer. Terriers come in a variety of sizes, but all are tough and have hard coats.

The purpose of the Toy Group is to delight dog owners, although toy dogs also sometimes served as hand or foot warmers. These small dogs include the Pug, Brussels Griffon, and Maltese.

The Herding Group is the newest group, made up of breeds who were originally part of the Working Group. Their job is herding flocks of sheep, cattle, or ducks. Most are larger dogs with a smooth gait that enables them to trot all day. Representatives of this group include the Pembroke Welsh Corgi, Briard, German Shepherd Dog, and Border Collie.

In addition, there is a Miscellaneous Group that contains breeds whose national clubs are working toward AKC recognition. (See appendix A for a complete list of AKC breeds.)

When you start thinking about which breeds may be right for you, the biggest mistake people make is choosing a breed based on its appearance. You may like the look of an Afghan Hound, but did you know they require *hours* of grooming every week? You may see an adorable Parson Russell Terrier on television, but this high-energy breed needs loads of attention and exercise. Think about the dog's characteristics *first*, before you consider his looks. Here are some questions you should ask yourself and your family.

What Level of Activity Do You Want in a Dog?

Is the dog you want reserved, energetic, or hyper? Perhaps you are an avid hiker or jogger and want a dog who will accompany you on family outings. Maybe your kids spend hours every day in the yard playing with their friends, and a dog could join them. Or perhaps you just like an enthusiastic dog. In my household, food does not hit the floor because it is intercepted before it ever gets that far!

Some breeds, such as Border Collies, have a high activity level, which can make them very difficult to live with. They are extremely intelligent and must be kept busy. Border Collies like to herd, whether it is a flock of sheep or a tennis ball rolling across the floor. While watching a human-Border Collie team in the sport of agility, it is quite evident that most people cannot get their commands out fast enough to keep up with these dogs. However, seeing such a team in harmony is a real treat.

On the other hand, you may want a quieter, calmer dog. Don't think every high-energy puppy will calm down into a low-energy dog. Yes, puppies

These Golden Retrievers are good buddies.

do get a bit less active as they grow up, but an active dog will always be active. If you want a less active dog, you need to choose a less active breed.

While some breeds are content to sleep on a rug in the corner of the room, other breeds demand to sleep on your pillow. Even on a cloudy day, I always have a "dog shadow" who sometimes trips me. One of my friends calls it the "umbilical cord syndrome" because it is very hard for me to walk out the door without having a parade in tow. When I sit down, the dogs all have to touch me, whether it is with a foot, head, or leg. For some people, this behavior is just fine, but for others it would be annoying.

Luckily, most breeds fall somewhere in between. With appropriate exercise, their exuberance can be handled quite nicely. Vigorous exercise several times a week will usually work wonders. Then there are breeds bred to take orders, such as retrievers and working breeds. For the most part, they seem calmer, but make no mistake, these dogs also need a good amount of exercise to keep healthy and burn off excess energy.

Are You Looking for a Dog for a Specific Purpose?

If you feel you need a guard dog, check the Working and Herding Groups, because dogs in those groups were bred to be protectors.

If your child wants to compete in agility trials, you might want to look at breeds who leave the dust flying and weave poles snapping, such as a Border Collie, Shetland Sheepdog, or Golden Retriever. If your child doesn't run very fast, a Welsh Corgi or Dachshund might be a better fit. If you want a breed that will be more manageable in the agility ring, consider a Miniature Poodle or one of the sturdier toy breeds, such as a Papillon or Cavalier King Charles Spaniel. If you want to compete in obedience, remember that dogs in the Hound and Toy Groups tend to have a mind of their own. Yoo are better off picking a breed that was developed to work on command, such as a dog from the Working Group or a retriever. Knowing your needs is important so that the breed you decide on fits your requirements.

What about the Coat?

Coat textures range from curly to wiry, hairless to long, double-coated to single-coated. Each coat type requires a different sort of maintenance. Coats were developed to suit the sort of work the breed does. A German Shorthaired Pointer's coat is short because he works in fields that contain burrs and thorns. Labrador and Golden Retrievers bring back game downed by the hunter, often in the cold water, so their double coats insulate them from freezing water and temperatures.

Think about how much time you are willing to spend grooming your dog. Then consult with the breeder about what is required for proper coat maintenance, including what equipment you will need to buy. For some breeds, it may be nothing more than a weekly nail trimming and brushing, while other breeds may require brushing several times a week or even daily.

There may also be other special needs related to a breed's coat. Breeds with little or no hair, such as the Chinese Crested, don't need a lot of grooming, but they do need special care. They can sunburn easily in the summer and suffer frostbite very quickly in the winter months. Other breeds, such as the Old English Sheepdog, have hair covering their eyes to protect them from bright sunlight. They can see through the hair the way you can see through window blinds, so there is no need to tie the hair back, because their eyes are sensitive to light and tying back the hair back may cause their eyes to tear.

Bathing is another issue. Too much bathing can cause skin problems; not enough will result in a dog with odors. Part of your decision should be based on the amount of time you have to properly care for your dog's coat. If you travel frequently and don't have a lot of time to make a coat shine, your Yorkshire Terrier will have to be drastically trimmed, thus losing the beautiful coat that highlights the breed.

Dalmatians have short hair, but this doesn't mean they don't shed.

Also be sure to find out about shedding. While every dog sheds to some extent, some certainly shed more than others. And some double-coated breeds, including the German Shepherd, Siberian Husky, and Alaskan Malamute, shed seasonally in a twice-annual ritual that breeders call "blowing coat." Make sure you understand how much dog hair you will have to vacuum up around your home before you pick a breed.

What's the Best Size Dog for You?

This is an important question. Dogs come in a variety of sizes, ranging from very small, such as Chihuahuas, to very large, such as Irish Wolfhounds, and many breeds in between. If your living accommodations are not large, a midsize dog would probably best suit your needs.

One of the most confusing issues parents face is what size dog is best for their children. Several factors must be kept in mind for both the safety of your child and of the dog. First is the age of your child. If you have a spunky six year old, you might want to pass on breeds that are delicately built, such as Whippets, and very small dogs, such as Yorkshire Terriers, Miniature Pinschers, and other toy breeds; a child's roughhousing can easily injure a delicately built dog. A playful little slap can end up being a broken leg for a tiny dog. However, a large breed such as a Newfoundland is not always the answer, either. A dog like this grows so big that he can accidentally hurt the child during playtime. A young child might be better paired with a breed that has more substance and is sturdier, even if the dog is small, such as a Beagle or Shetland Sheepdog.

A twelve-year-old child can easily get along with a larger dog, because he is big enough to protect himself from being knocked over.

A common mistake people make is not researching the size of the breed at maturity. A little Bernese Mountain Dog puppy looks like an adorable teddy bear, but he can grow to twenty-seven inches tall at the shoulder and weigh ninety-plus pounds. Will that be too much dog for you?

Responsible breeders will tell you the pros and cons of the breed, which include the size and weight of an adult animal. An eight-week-old puppy may play happily with your child, but things may be quite different in a few weeks, when the pup has grown. If the cute puppy you brought home is a Labrador Retriever, in a few weeks he may outweigh the child, and what was playful behavior then may be harmful now.

How Is This Breed with Children?

Size is one aspect of this question. So is activity level. Kids like to play with their dog, and that includes running, throwing balls, wrestling, swimming, and lots of other activities. Bulldogs and other short-faced breeds may not be able to keep up with most kids.

Some breeds are particularly sensitive to sound, and the high-pitched, loud voices of children may inspire fear or even aggression in those breeds. Some are sensitive to quick movements, which could also make them poor choices for families with children. Some of the herding breeds, particularly the short-legged ones, are bred to control livestock by nipping at their heels and may try to control your children that way as well.

Another important thing to find out is how independent the breed is in general. A breed that is independent, such as many of the sighthounds, may not be as good a playmate as a breed that is very people-oriented.

Take a look at the section in the breed standard that describes temperament. You want to avoid a breed that is described as sharp, guarded, or suspicious of strangers. Your dog not only has to be friendly and safe with your kids, but with all the friends they bring home as well.

Are Some Breeds Healthier Than Others?

The general health of a dog is based on his genetics, his environment (including veterinary care, nutrition, and exercise), and chance. While each dog is an individual and each dog's circumstances are different, there are specific health problems that lurk in the gene pools of certain breeds. This doesn't mean every dog of that breed will have that health problem, but it does mean the dog is more likely to have them. So as you consider which breed to get, one of the questions you should ask is, What health problems occur in this breed? (Some of the more common health problems will be discussed later in this chapter.)

Some breeds are more prone than others to develop hip dysplasia or eye problems. Some dogs may develop a lifelong problem such as epilepsy, which requires drugs to keep seizures to a minimum, or diabetes, which requires insulin shots. These drugs can be expensive, so you need to know whether your finances can stretch to pay for daily medications that would have to be given to the dog for the rest of his life.

If the thought of an expensive health problem that requires diagnostic work or surgery scares you, be sure to choose a breed that is known to be generally healthy. On the other hand, one of the most vet-intensive of all breeds is the English Bulldog, which is prone to cherry eye, soft palate problems, and various other diseases. Yet, the breed has a loyal following, and thousands of people bring these adorable puppies into their homes every year.

How Do You Research the Breeds?

Now that you have a list of attributes you want in a dog, how do you find out which breeds fit the bill? The AKC Web site (www.akc.org) describes all the breeds it recognizes, and includes a picture of each dog. There are also numerous dog books that describe the attributes of dozens of breeds (two good ones are A Perfect Match by Chris Walkowicz and The New Encyclopedia of the Dog by Dr. Bruce Fogle). You can sit back, thumb through the pages, and mark the ones that interest you. One book your children may enjoy is The Complete Dog Book for Kids, a publication of the AKC.

When you have narrowed your choice down a bit, start looking deeper. Every breed has a national club, and most have a Web site (they are listed in appendix B). There also are breed-specific books on just about every dog breed.

Read the Breed Standard

Every breed has a breed standard, a point-by-point description of the physical attributes and temperament of the perfect dog of that breed. While there is no such thing as a perfect dog, breeders use the standard as a guide in their breeding programs. Judges also use it to evaluate

Jake holds his dog Freddy, a smooth Brussels Griffon.

the dogs in conformation shows (while it may seem as if the dogs in the ring are simply being compared to one another, in reality they are all being compared against the breed standard).

The breed standard is written by the national breed club, using guidelines established by the registry that recognizes the breed (such as the AKC or the United Kennel Club). You can find breed standards at the Web site of the national registry or the national breed club. Many books also print the breed standards. The standards do change from time to time, so make sure you are reading the most recent edition of a book.

The first section of the breed standard gives you a brief overview of the breed's history and origins. It describes the breed's original purpose, which will tell you a lot about the dog's temperament—hunting dogs tend to be active and take direction well, herding dogs tend to be protective, fighting dogs tend to be tenacious and stubborn, companion dogs tend to crave more company, and so on. The standard then describes the breed's general appearance (short and sturdy, long and elegant, etc.) and the dog's size as an adult. There will be some variation by sex; males tend to be a bit larger than females in most breeds.

Next comes a detailed description of the head and neck, then the back and body, and then the front and rear legs. The section on coat will describe the ideal coat, including how the dog should be presented in the show ring. A section on color and markings describes all acceptable—and unacceptable—colors, patterns, and markings. Then there's a section that describes how the dog moves, called *gait*. A dog's gait reveals a great deal about the soundness of his internal structure, so it's worthwhile to study this section carefully. Finally, there will be a section on temperament, which it is also wise to read very carefully. Conscientious breeders take the entire standard very seriously, including temperament, and if the standard calls for a dog who is reserved and guarded, this is probably not be the right dog for a family.

In every section of the standard, the description of ideal traits is followed by a list of characteristics that are considered to be faults (undesirable qualities) or disqualifications, which means the dog should not be shown in conformation nor should it be bred. These faults and disqualifications usually came about because of the original work the dog was bred to do. For example, a Bloodhound with small ears would not be able to

Good Advice for Parents

I always tell parents that *they* have to want the dog, or at the very least *they* have to be prepared to do all the work and spend all the money because, although it would be great if they can teach their child responsibility by making him or her at least partially responsible for the dog, it isn't fair to the animal to make its well-being dependent on the responsibility and reliability of a child—up to and including a 17-year-old child.

In other words, they can tell the child, "It's your job to take Bosco out for his morning walk before school," but if the child doesn't do it for any reason (and they won't), the parents have to be fully prepared to do it themselves.

Also, the dog should not become a point of constant conflict between parent and child, and parents should not set up expectations in the beginning that are likely to make it so.

In most cases, however, what I find is that the parent really does want the dog themselves, and they are using the child as an excuse—kind of like going to the circus with your child when you might be embarrassed to go yourself.

—An experienced breeder of Belgian Malinois

follow scent. If you want a pet dog and not a working dog, these faults may not be important to you. It is the superficial faults in a dog's appearance that often distinguishes a pet-quality puppy from a show- or competition-quality puppy. A Vizsla with a splash of white on his neck is one example. However, some faults and disqualifications are structural and affect the way a dog moves or his overall health. And faults in temperament are serious business.

Breed standards are not easy to read because they use a lot of specialized language, but it's worth the effort. Pull out your dictionary, or look in your local library for a copy of *Canine Terminology* by Howard Spira. Most books about individual breeds also contain explanations of what the standard means. Understanding what is and is not acceptable in the breed will help you understand exactly what kind of dog this breed is, how big he gets, how he moves, and how you will need to care for him. It will also help you identify responsible breeders (more on this in chapter 5) because reputable breeders will not use dogs with disqualifying traits and will weed out dogs with major and serious faults from their breeding program. They take the standard seriously and always try to breed dogs that measure up. If a breeder offers you "rare" dogs with multicolor markings (called parti-color) and you know the standard says only solid colors are allowed for that breed, she's trying to put one past you.

Dog Events and Family Pet Shows

Dog shows, field trials, agility trials, family pet shows, and club-sponsored events are terrific places to be introduced to the breeds you have been researching. Many large cities, such New York, Detroit, Chicago, Houston, and various cities in California, host dog shows in which the dogs are on display for you and your family to see, meet, and talk with their owners and handlers. These are called benched shows.

At these shows you will see dogs being judged by how well they conform to the breed standard. Dog shows often have obedience and agility competitions as well, various kinds of demonstrations, and other fun activities. Even when shows are not benched, the people who are showing their dogs often stick around for most of the day, socializing with other breeders. It's perfectly okay to wander around the area where the dogs are kept and ask questions about a breed. Most breeders will be delighted to answer your questions. Just don't touch any dog without first asking permission.

Puppy or Adult Dog?

There are pros and cons to each. Puppies are cute, cuddly, and loads of fun, but also lots of work. A puppy needs housebreaking and training. Puppies are very demanding of your time. Just ask anyone who has gone through the experience! On the other hand, raising a puppy can be a very rewarding experience because you are with him through all the stages of growth.

Older dogs are usually more settled, housebroken, and past the chewing stage, and many have had some type of obedience training, whether formal or informal. An older dog is usually a better fit with young children because these dogs are usually less demanding, less likely to jump up, and more easy to fit into your existing routine. In addition, the cost can be significantly less. Whether a dog is young or old, he will still do what a dog is supposed to do—provide companionship.

A Little Bit about Genetics

It's important to talk to every breeder about health problems in the breed and what they are doing to avoid them. The specific genes that trigger some congenital health problems (those that are present at birth) are known, and tests have been developed to detect these genes. For other problems, such as hip and elbow dysplasia, physical signs will point to the probability of these problems occurring in a dog's offspring. Testing both parents before they are bred can help ward off these types of problems, although it is no guarantee.

While it's important to remember that no breeder, no matter how conscientious, can breed 100 percent healthy puppies 100 percent of the time. A breeder who knows what problems lurk in her breed's gene pool and does all she can to breed away from them is the one you want a puppy from. Any breeder who tells you that her breed has no health concerns or that none of her dogs have ever had a health problem is not being forthright with you, and you are better off getting a dog from someone else.

Educated breeders know a lot about genetics and what the various breed lines or "family trees" produce. So when you talk to a breeder about her breeding program, she may use a lot of terms that you only vaguely recall from high school biology. Here's a quick refresher course.

Inbreeding

Inbreeding means breeding animals who are closely related to one another—parent to offspring (sometimes called a backcross) or full brother to full sister. Some breeders also refer to matings between a grandsire and his granddaughter as inbreeding, although some geneticists would disagree with this definition.

Acording to Elizabeth Becker, a professor of biology, inbreeding offers benefits and drawbacks. It increases the likelihood of reproducing certain desirable traits, but it also greatly increases the chance of reproducing undesirable traits. A common misconception is that all inbred dogs are unhealthy or have poor temperament, but this is not the case. It is not the inbreeding but the genetic potential in closely related individuals that determines the health and temperament of the puppies. Inbreeding two genetically sound individuals will produce genetically sound puppies. The problem is that any unknown genetic problems that lurk in a line will show up more quickly in inbred individuals. This is why you need to work with experienced breeders who know the background both in health and temperament of the dogs they breed.

For breeders who understand pedigrees and genetics and have a good knowledge of the problems within a given line, a limited amount of cautious inbreeding may prove helpful. But in general, inbreeding is avoided because it increases the potential for disease or temperament problems.

Line Breeding

Line breeding means breeding animals who are related through a common ancestor, but not directly. Skillful line breeding is an excellent way to strengthen a desirable quality in a litter. For instance, a breeder may be trying to breed dogs with a certain look so that her dogs will be successful in the show ring. Or possibly a breeder wants to breed dogs for a specific performance skill, such as better speed, agility, or hunting or herding instincts. By looking at a dog's pedigree (which is simply a record of who his ancestors were), breeders can study the type of work they did, the titles they earned, and, in more recent generations, the health problems that have been documented, and select a sire and a dam who are mostly likely to produce the desired characteristics without the extra risk of problems posed by inbreeding.

Outcrossing

Outcrossing means breeding unrelated animals. By outcrossing, breeders increase the genetic variation in their dogs and minimize the risks of inbreeding problems. This is usually the safest breeding strategy because it keeps variation in the gene pool. Some of the problem genes may still be there (especially if a specific problem is common in the entire breed), but it increases the likelihood of a puppy inheriting healthy genes from at least one parent, so problems can be kept to a minimum.

Sometimes one dog just isn't enough!

However, outcrossing does make it more difficult to predict the specific physical type and sporting abilities of each resulting puppy. Breeders using two good dogs who are unrelated (or, in the case of a breed with a small population, only distantly related) will have a good chance of getting good puppies within a range representing the strong and weak points of the dogs involved.

Among purebred dog breeders, outcrossing means breeding unrelated animals of the same breed. But outcrosses have also been used between breeds, to develop new breeds, to emphasize a specific characteristic in a dog, or to help eliminate health problems such as deafness in a breed. This kind of outcross does not produce a purebred dog, but for some dog breeders that is not important. Many mushers outcross their dogs to get top sled dogs and hunters sometimes mix dogs of different breeds to get a dog with the specific hunting skills they desire. Many champion performance hunter and jumper horses are outcrosses between different breeds of horse. Take a draft horse and cross it with a Thoroughbred and you will, hopefully, get a horse with strength, size, thicker bones, and even temperament from the draft parent and the speed, good looks, and heart of the Thoroughbred.

Medical Problems Commonly Found in Dogs

Unfortunately, no breed of dog is free of health problems. Some problems are minor, while others can be fatal. Responsible breeders try to eliminate problems in their breed through both appropriate certifications and selective breeding. The following are sixteen somewhat common conditions, along with the breeds most prone to them. *This does not mean every dog of that breed has this health problem, or that dogs of other breeds never have this health problem.* It does mean you must ask the dog's breeder what she is doing to breed away from health problems in her lines. Although breeding isn't an exact science, at least when you're working with a breeder who does the appropriate certifications and health screenings, you have a better chance of getting a healthy animal.

Most national breed clubs have more information on these and other canine health problems on their Web sites (see appendix B).

Bloat

Bloat is actually two conditions: gastric dilation, in which the stomach distends with gas and fluid, and volvulus or torsion, in which the

These are very healthy English Cocker Spaniel puppies.

distended stomach rotates on its long axis. It occurs most commonly in large, deep-chested dogs. Bloat can be fatal and requires immediately veterinary attention and sometimes surgery. Feeding your dog frequent, smaller meals and postponing hard exercise for one hour after eating is suggested for deep-chested dogs. The breeds most often prone to bloat are:

Akita	Great Pyrenees
Alaskan Malamute	Greyhound
Beauceron	Irish Setter
Bernese Mountain Dog	Irish Wolfhound
Collie	Newfoundland
Dachshund	Otterhound
German Shepherd Dog	Poodle
Golden Retriever	Samoyed
Gordon Setter	Scottish Deerhound
Great Dane	Weimaraner

Cancer

Osteosarcoma, hemangiosarcoma, lymphoma, breast, mast cell tumors, and brain tumors occur with greater frequency in the breeds in the following list. Osteosarcoma is bone cancer. Hemangiosarcoma is a malignant tumor of the blood vessels and can occur in the skin, liver, spleen, muscles, or heart. Lymphoma is cancer of the lymph nodes. Mast cell tumors are found on the skin, and about half are malignant.

Afghan Hound	Boxer
Akita	Bullmastiff
American Water Spaniel	Irish Setter
Australian Terrier	Norwegian Elkhound
Beagle	Skye Terrier
Bernese Mountain Dog	Vizsla
Borzoi	Welsh Springer Spaniel
Boston Terrier	

Deafness

Dogs used in breeding programs should have a Brainstem Auditory Evoked Response (BAER) test (see chapter 5) to certify they are free of this problem, if it is a breed problem.

Beagle	Havanese
Boston Terrier	Ibizan Hound
Bull Terrier	Parson Russell Terrier
Chinese Crested	Smooth Fox Terrier
Dalmatian	Wire Fox Terrier
English Setter	

Ectropian

Ectropion is a condition in which the lower eyelid rolls out from the eye, exposing it to irritants. It gives the eye a droopy appearance, and occurs in dogs with loose skin on the face, such as scenthounds and spaniels. The breeds most often prone to ectropian are:

Beauceron	Golden Retriever
Bernese Mountain Dog	Shih Tzu
Bulldog	St. Bernard
Curly-Coated Retriever	Welsh Springer Spaniel

Elbow Dysplasia

Elbow dysplasia is an inherited defect of the elbow joint and a common cause of front-leg lameness and decreased range of motion in large dogs. If the condition is serious, it can cause the dog much pain. Dogs used in breeding programs should be certified free of this disorder, if it is a breed problem. The breeds most often prone to elbow dysplasia are:

Akita	Curly-Coated Retriever
Basset Hound	German Shepherd Dog
Belgian Sheepdog	Giant Schnauzer
Belgian Tervuren	Irish Wolfhound
Bernese Mountain Dog	Labrador Retriever
Black and Tan Coonhound	Neapolitan Mastiff
Bloodhound	Newfoundland
Bouvier des Flandres	Nova Scotia Duck Tolling Retriever
Brittany	
Bullmastiff	Puli
Chinese Shar-Pei	Rhodesian Ridgeback
Chow Chow	Tibetan Terrier

Entropian

Entropian, sometimes called diamond eye, is a congenital defect in which the eyelids roll inward, causing irritation and tearing and sometimes corneal abrasions. It is painful and a dog can eventually go blind from scarring. This problem can be surgically corrected. The breeds most often prone to entropian are:

Beauceron	Bulldog
Bernese Mountain Dog	Chinese Shar-Pei

Chow Chow   Poodle
Curly-Coated Retriever   Pug
Golden Retriever   Vizsla
Great Pyrenees   Weimaraner
Irish Water Spaniel   Welsh Springer Spaniel
Newfoundland

Epilepsy and Seizures

In dogs as in humans, epilepsy is a misfiring of the neurons in the brain that causes involuntary contractions of the muscles—seizures. A seizure can be as mild as the dog staring into space or as severe as grand mal epilepsy. Epilepsy is diagnosed when all other problems that could cause seizures have been eliminated, so often in dogs the cause of the epilepsy is unknown. The breeds most often prone to seizures are:

American Water Spaniel   Ibizan Hound
Australian Terrier   Irish Water Spaniel
Belgian Tervuren   Irish Wolfhound
Border Collie   Italian Greyhound
Border Terrier   Japanese Chin
Borzoi   Keeshond
Boston Terrier   Labrador Retriever
Brittany   Manchester Terrier
Cairn Terrier   Miniature Pinscher
Chinese Crested   Newfoundland
Clumber Spaniel   Norfolk Terrier
Collie   Otterhound
Dachshund   Pomeranian
Dalmatian   Poodle
English Cocker Spaniel   Pug
French Bulldog   Rottweiler
Harrier   Saluki

Schipperke   Vizsla

Scottish Terrier   Welsh Springer Spaniel

Shetland Sheepdog   Welsh Terrier

St. Bernard

Eye Disorders

Glaucoma, corneal ulcers, distichiasis, lens luxation, cataracts, and corneal dystrophy occur with greater frequency in the breeds in the following list. Glaucoma occurs when fluid in the eye is produced faster than it can be removed, leading to a build up of pressure within the eye. It is a hereditary disease that affects Beagles, Basset Hounds, Cocker Spaniels, Samoyeds, and other breeds. Corneal ulcers are deep abrasions on the surface of the cornea. A specific type of slow-healing ulcer is found in Boxers, Samoyeds, Dachshunds, Miniature Poodles, Pembroke Welsh Corgis, Wire Fox Terriers, and Shetland Sheepdogs. Distichiasis, or double eyelashes, is an extra row of eyelashes usually found on the lower lid and occasionally found on the upper lid, which leads to abrasions of the cornea. Lens luxation is the abnormal position of the lens in the eye. A cataract is an opacity of the lens of the eye, causing impairment of vision or blindness. Corneal dystrophy is a general term that refers to diseases and scarring of the cornea. Dogs used in breeding programs should be certified free of eye problems, if it is a breed problem.

American Eskimo Dog   Bouvier des Flandres

Australian Terrier   Brittany

Basenji   Cairn Terrier

Beagle   Chinese Crested

Bearded Collie   Chow Chow

Belgian Sheepdog   Dandie Dinmont Terrier

Bichon Frise   English Toy Spaniel

Bloodhound   Golden Retriever

Border Collie   Great Dane

Borzoi   Ibizan Hound

Japanese Chin

Kerry Blue Terrier

Labrador Retriever

Miniature Bull Terrier

Miniature Pinscher

Neapolitan Mastiff

Petit Basset Griffon
    Vendeen

Pomeranian

Poodle

Pug

Rhodesian Ridgeback

Scottish Deerhound

Shih Tzu

Staffordshire Bull Terrier

Tibetan Terrier

Welsh Springer Spaniel

Welsh Terrier

Whippet

Wire Fox Terrier

Heart Problems

Congenital heart disease is any heart problem that is inherited. Various congenital heart diseases, including cardiomyopathy, endocardiosis, chronic obstructive pulmonary disease (COPD), aortic stenosis, aortic or subaortic valvular stenosis, heart murmurs, and congenital heart failure occur with greater frequency in the breeds in the following list.

Cardiomyopathy is a disease of the heart muscle characterized by heart enlargement and dysfunction. It is common in Boxers, Doberman Pinschers, and many other breeds. Infectious endocarditis is caused by a bacterial infection of the heart valves or lining of the heart, which weakens them. It is often fatal. COPD results when the rings of the branches in the lungs become inflamed and obstruct breathing. It can lead to increased back pressure to the heart. Stenosis of the aorta or of the aortic or subaortic valves is a condition resulting from restriction of the flow of blood leaving the heart, which forces other parts to work too hard. A heart murmur is any abnormal heart sound created by turbulent blood flow through the heart (not to be confused with arrhythmia, which is an interruption in the regular rhythmic heartbeat). Congenital heart failure is a condition marked by weakness, swelling, and shortness of breath caused by inadequate blood circulation.

American Water Spaniel

Basenji

Basset Hound

Border Terrier

Borzoi

Boxer

Brittany

Bull Terrier

Cairn Terrier

Curly-Coated Retriever

Doberman Pinscher

English Toy Spaniel

French Bulldog

Golden Retriever

Havanese

Irish Wolfhound

Japanese Chin

Keeshond

Manchester Terrier

Neapolitan Mastiff

Nova Scotia Duck Tolling Retriever

Parson Russell Terrier

Shiba Inu

Hip Dysplasia

Hip dysplasia is a congenital deformity of the hip joints, and ranges from mild to crippling. When it becomes severe, it causes lameness and requires the attention of a veterinarian. Treatment might include pain medications, surgery, a combination of both, or, in the most severe cases, euthanasia.

Breeders should receive clearances from the Orthopedic Foundation for Animals (OFA) or the University of Pennsylvania Hip Improvement Program (PennHIP) before breeding dogs of any breed known to have this problem (see chapter 6). The breeds most often prone to hip dysplasia are:

Affenpinscher

Airedale

Akita

Alaskan Malamute

Australian Cattle Dog

Basenji

Bearded Collie

Beauceron

Belgian Malinois

Belgian Sheepdog

Bernese Mountain Dog

Black and Tan Coonhound

Bloodhound

Border Terrier

Borzoi

Bouvier des Flandres

Boxer

Brittany

Briard

Bullmastiff

Bulldog

Chinese Shar-Pei

Chow Chow

Clumber Spaniel

Curly-Coated Retriever

Dalmatian

Doberman Pinscher

English Cocker Spaniel

English Springer Spaniel

German Pinscher

German Shepherd Dog

Giant Schnauzer

Glen of Imaal Terrier

Golden Retriever

Gordon Setter

Great Dane

Great Pyrenees

Havanese

Irish Setter

Irish Water Spaniel

Irish Wolfhound

Keeshond

Kuvasz

Labrador Retriever

Lowchen

Mastiff

Miniature Pinscher

Newfoundland

Nova Scotia Duck Tolling Retriever

Old English Sheepdog

Otterhound

Parson Russell Terrier

Pharaoh Hound

Poodle

Portuguese Water Dog

Pug

Puli

Rhodesian Ridgeback

Rottweiler

Samoyed

Scottish Deerhound

Shiba Inu

St. Bernard

Staffordshire Bull Terrier

Tibetan Terrier

Vizsla

Weimaraner

Welsh Springer Spaniel

West Highland White Terrier

Hypothyroidism

Hypothyroidism is inadequate output of thyroid hormones. This affects a dog's coat, general metabolism, electrolyte balance, and other body systems. Signs in affected dogs include lethargy, obesity, mental dullness, and irregular heat cycles. The breeds most often prone to hypothyroidism are:

Basset Hound	English Cocker Spaniel
Beagle	Gordon Setter
Bearded Collie	Great Dane
Boxer	Irish Water Spaniel
Bouvier des Flandres	Irish Wolfhound
Bull Terrier	Neapolitan Mastiff
Cairn Terrier	Petit Basset Griffon Vendeen
Chinese Shar-Pei	Poodle
Clumber Spaniel	Rottweiler
Dachshund	Vizsla
Dalmatian	Weimaraner
Doberman Pinscher	Welsh Terrier

Legg-Perthes Disease

Legg-Perthes disease is caused by the death of bone tissue on the head of the femur (thigh bone) resulting from an interruption in the blood supply. It occurs most often in small-breed puppies between four and eleven months of age. Dogs used in breeding programs should be certified free of this disorder, if it is a breed problem. The breeds most often prone to Legg-Perthes disease are:

Affenpinscher	Manchester Terrier
Cairn Terrier	Miniature Pinscher
Lakeland Terrier	Poodle

Pug   Toy Fox Terrier

Smooth Fox Terrier   West Highland White Terrier

Luxating Patella

The patella (kneecap) luxates when it pops out of place, either to the inside or the outside of the knee joint. When it slips to the inside, it's called medial luxation, and this is more common in toy breeds. When the kneecap slips to the outside, it's called lateral luxation, and this condition is more common in large and giant breeds. Dogs used in breeding programs should be certified free of this disorder, if it is a breed problem. The breeds most often prone to luxating patella are:

Affenpinscher	French Bulldog
American Eskimo Dog	Great Pyrenees
Australian Terrier	Havanese
Basset Hound	Keeshond
Bichon Frise	Lakeland Terrier
Black and Tan Coonhound	Miniature Pinscher
Bloodhound	Petit Basset Griffon Vendeen
Border Terrier	Puli
Bull Terrier	Shiba Inu
Cairn Terrier	Tibetan Terrier
Chinese Shar-Pei	Toy Fox Terrier
English Toy Spaniel	West Highland White Terrier
Finnish Spitz	

Progressive Retinal Atrophy

Progressive retinal atrophy (PRA) occurs in different forms in different breeds, but in all cases there is destruction of the retinal cells in both eyes, leading to blindness. There is no treatment. Dogs who have been screened for PRA can be listed in the Canine Eye Registration Foundation (CERF), thus enabling breeders to avoid the disease in their lines (see chapter 6). Dogs should be tested before breeding to make sure they are free of eye problems, if it is a breed problem. The breeds most often prone to PRA are:

Akita	English Cocker Spaniel
Alaskan Malamute	English Springer Spaniel
Australian Cattle Dog	Glen of Imaal Terrier
Basenji	Golden Retriever
Belgian Tervuren	Irish Wolfhound
Bernese Mountain Dog	Labrador Retriever
Borzoi	Lhasa Apso
Boston Terrier	Lowchen
Briard	Miniature Schnauzer
Bullmastiff	Old English Sheepdog
Cairn Terrier	Poodle
Cardigan Welsh Corgi	Samoyed
Chinese Crested	Shiba Inu
Collie	Shih Tzu
Curly-Coated Retriever	Siberian Husky
Dachshund	Tibetan Terrier
Doberman Pinscher	

Von Willebrand's Disease

Von Willebrand's disease is the most common inherited bleeding disorder in dogs. The bleeding is caused by a deficiency of a specific plasma protein called the von Willebrand factor. Dogs used in breeding programs should be tested before breeding to make sure they are free of the disease. The breeds most often prone to von Willebrand's disease are:

Basset Hound

Bernese Mountain Dog

Bullmastiff

Cairn Terrier

Collie

Doberman Pinscher

Irish Wolfhound

Keeshond

Lakeland Terrier

Manchester Terrier

Newfoundland

Poodle

Scottish Terrier

Vizsla

Weimaraner

5

Where Will You Find Your Dog?

Where can you get a good, sound, healthy dog? There are several options, some better than others, whether you're looking for a puppy or an adult dog. The best places to get a dog are from responsible and reputable breeders, local shelters, and breed rescue organizations. Less good places are pet shops, puppy mills, and backyard breeders. You can look for breeders in newspapers, dog magazines, and on the Internet, and it's also a good idea to do some research at dog shows and sporting events. It is very important that wherever you decide to get your dog, you choose carefully. Check the references of everyone, whether they're a breeder, rescue group, or shelter. People advertising dogs on the Internet are becoming especially savvy in their selling techniques and have learned the right answers to give you, so checking references is very important. You need to remember that this dog will be a family member for a decade or more. Here are some of the pros and cons of each of your choices.

Responsible Breeders

Responsible breeders are people who exhibit their dogs at dog shows and/or compete with them in canine sporting events, educate themselves about the hereditary and health problems of the breed, and work to eliminate these problems through careful and selective breeding. These are the breeders you should work with when searching for a purebred dog. They test all dogs used in their breeding program for hereditary health problems, and eliminate questionable animals from their breeding stock by spaying or neutering them. They only use dogs in their breeding program who have received health clearances through testing.

In addition, the dogs they breed meet the breed standard. These breeders are familiar with what characteristics the various lines of a family tree produce in their offspring. They have a good idea of whether the dogs are likely to produce offspring who are big-boned, large or small, as well as other attributes such as birdiness (the desire to hunt and retrieve game birds) in hunting dogs, speed in sighthounds, or good herding ability in shepherds.

In case a problem does occur, most breeders offer health guarantees. These guarantees, which should be in writing, give the breeder the option of either replacing the puppy, returning your money, or making a contribution toward corrective medical procedures, such as surgery to repair a hernia or helping to defray the cost of hip surgery. Even the best breeders occasionally have a problem with a puppy, but it is the responsible breeder who takes corrective measures to assist you and the puppy.

Responsible breeders are a resource for you and your dog. Your dog's breeder should be the first person you consult with about any problem. Perhaps the breeder can solve the problem very quickly, or she may refer you to an expert for assistance. Keep your breeder involved, because good breeders want to know what is happening with every puppy they breed. She may be able to save you the time and expense of a visit to the veterinarian. As an example, one woman worried that her Brussels Griffon puppy had a runny nose. She called the breeder, who assured her that runny noses are common in young puppies of that brachycephalic (short-nosed) breed and not necessarily a sign of a problem. The breeder told her what symptoms *would* indicate a problem, such as listlessness or refusing food and water.

Occasionally, due to unforeseen reasons, families must give up their dog. Responsible breeders will take the dog back and/or help you find a suitable new family for him. Before you purchase a puppy, ask what the breeder's policy is on this matter and get it in writing. (For more on what to ask your dog's breeder, see chapter 6.)

If you are looking for an older companion, sometimes a breeder will have a dog who may be suitable for your family. She may have a dog who is retiring from competition and breeding. She may have a dog who was

The Story of Mr. Johnson

One story comes to mind as an example of what you do *not* want to happen to your family.

Mr. Johnson decided to surprise his eight-year-old son with a puppy. He went to the pet shop and picked out a very cute, six-week-old Golden Retriever, whom his son named Ruby.

Several days after the puppy came home, Ruby became very ill. After an emergency visit to a veterinarian and several expensive laboratory tests, Ruby was diagnosed with parvovirus (a serious infection of the gastrointestinal tract), which was complicated by a heart condition. Ruby died two days later. The family was devastated.

What could Mr. Johnson have done differently? Could he have prevented this disaster? Although Mr. Johnson's heart was in the right place, his family suffered a horrible and unforgettable experience.

This doesn't have to happen to you. It is an avoidable situation, if you use the lessons in this book.

returned because of a divorce or a move by the original owner. This can be an excellent way to get a quality dog at a reasonable price.

Responsible breeders do not sell puppies to pet shops; if they do, they risk their reputation among their peers. Furthermore, many local and national clubs have a Code of Ethics that breeders agree to when they join. They agree to certify their breeding stock to be free of health-related issues in the breed, and they will not sell puppies to pet shops.

Where Can You Find a Responsible Breeder?

The best way to contact responsible breeders in your area is through national and local breed club referrals. In appendix B you will find a list of all the national breed clubs associated with the American Kennel Club. Visit the breed club's Web site and you will receive all kinds of information about national events, health issues, health surveys, as well as contact information for the breeder referral and rescue chairs. Some sites even

Health Certifications

OFA—Orthopedic Foundation for Animals

PennHIP—University of Pennsylvania Hip Improvement Program

CERF—Canine Eye Registration Foundation

BAER—Brainstem Auditory Evoked Response

These certifications are more fully discussed in chapter 6.

break down the information into local areas for you. National clubs also maintain databases for health certifications.

When speaking with the national breeder referral contact, you may want to ask about the club's rescue program. Ask about when and where events such as dog shows or field trials will be held. Attending these events is a great way to not only talk with breeders from all over the country, but also to meet some of their dogs.

Local clubs hold activities of their own in their area, including specialties (a special dog show with other competitive events that is held just for that breed), special events at all-breed shows, obedience, agility, and whatever other events the dogs were originally bred for, such as field, lure coursing, etc. Many of the clubs hold picnics, fun days, and training days, all to help owners understand their dog and the breed better. These are all good places to meet local breeders and learn more about the breed. You may want to contact the local club to receive a calendar of events so that you can see dogs participating in various activities.

Rescue Groups

Rescue groups are a great source for dogs. If you are mostly interested in companionship and don't plan on showing, this could be the way to go. Dogs available though a rescue program come in all ages, but most are adult, healthy animals. The price is generally very reasonable. Rescue groups get their dogs from a variety of places and reasons, mostly due to

Those Funny Kennel Names

To identify their own line of dogs, breeders use kennel names. All the dogs from the same kennel have the same kennel name. Any sort of name can be a kennel name; there is no rule about how to create one. Someone who lives on Bellevue Street might decide to name his dog Bellevue's Princess, and her offspring might be Bellevue's Duke, Bellevue's King, and Bellevue's Baron.

Other people like to create kennel names from their own names: *Jerdon* Kennel might be a kennel owned by Jerry and Donna Smith. *Marsward* Kennel is owned by Marilyn S. Wardsley. *Parisfield* is a kennel owned by a woman whose favorite city is Paris.

After the kennel name comes the part of the dog's name that identifies him individually. Sometimes breeders will use a single theme to name all the puppies in a litter; this helps them remember which puppies are related. So, for example, a litter of pups from the Bellevue Kennel might all be named after flowers: Bellevue Rose, Bellevue Daisy, Bellevue Columbine, and Bellevue Aster. These are the pups' *registered names*.

Dogs also have *call names*, the short name by which they are known around the house. These are names such as Zip, Bucky, Billy, and Spot.

When it comes to naming your new dog, the American Kennel Club application for registration is very clear: only the owner of the dog chooses the name. Breeders often fill in their own kennel name as the first part of the dog's name. You might have the chance to fill in the rest of the dog's name, or the breeder may have already filled it in. It doesn't matter what the dog's official registered name is, though—the call name is always up to you.

job transfers, divorce, the owner's death, abandoned and lost dogs who have been brought to them, and dogs taken from area shelters.

Sometimes, the dogs end up in rescue because they have outsmarted their owners. I had one call over Christmas from a furious woman whose dog kicked the empty water dish as a way to ask for water and, when she

Dogs give us an excuse to play outside.

was filling it up, grabbed the dinner roast off the counter. She wanted to get rid of him immediately. Hopefully, when you get a dog, you will have more patience and train him to have better manners.

There are several types of rescue groups. Breed rescue groups specialize in one breed and network around their area and possibly the whole country to help find homes for the dogs in their program. Breed rescue group members are very knowledgeable about their breed.

Other organizations may work with a variety of dogs in a particular group, such as Working and Herding dogs, while still others work with dogs of any breed, including mixed-breed dogs. No matter which group they are affiliated with, rescue volunteers work hard. These people pick up dogs, get medical assistance for them, work with shelters and sometimes other rescue organizations, and find emergency foster homes for dogs—all as volunteers. The work is demanding and emotionally draining, but very rewarding when a dog is given a second chance that he might not have had without them. A very good reference about breed rescue is Liz Palika's book *Purebred Rescue Dog Adoption*.

Often, special care is needed to help an animal who has been neglected. Sometimes volunteers take in older dogs who may not be adoptable due to age or health problems and give them a home. Sometimes volunteers have to make that hard call to put a dog down who cannot be helped. This is gut-wrenching work, done out of love for animals.

Several years ago, shelters and breed rescue organizations did not work well with one another. Luckily, that has changed. Although some shelters still refuse to work with rescue groups, many shelters have found that working with these groups actually helps stretch their limited budget by removing adoptable purebred dogs, thus creating space for other needy animals. Since purebred rescue volunteers usually have families in their program who are waiting to adopt, their success in finding a dog an appropriate home is much higher. In essence, when the two groups work together, more dogs are saved.

When dogs come into a rescue program, they are evaluated using the information received from the owner, the foster home caregiver, and/or shelter personnel. Dogs are fostered for a period that will enable the volunteer to get an idea of how the dog fits in with their family, including other animals, and if there are any health concerns. This information becomes part of the dog's file, and then possible homes are identified.

The personalities of the dog and the prospective family are critical when placing a dog into a new home. Through the information collected from foster homes, owners, and other sources, the rescue organization can determine what type of home would be an ideal fit. Is the dog used to children? What ages? Does the dog get along with other dogs? Does the dog get along with cats? One rule of the rescue organization I worked with was that we would not displace one animal for the sake of another animal.

Sometimes, volunteers find that some dogs would benefit from being placed with a family that has had the breed before. Armed with this information, volunteers contact only those kinds of prospective homes for this particular dog.

A rescue group will require you to fill out an application form, which will have questions concerning your lifestyle, interest and experience with the breed, family, and past pet history. You will be asked questions such as:

Why do you want this particular breed?

Have you had this breed before?

If so, where did you get your dog?

What happened with your last dog?

Was it a pet or show dog?

Did you compete?

Did you breed that dog?

Do you have other pets? If so, what kind?

Are you sure your living arrangements can accommodate this dog?

Is your yard fenced?

Are you prepared to walk the dog and make sure he gets adequate exercise?

If you live in an apartment, will your lease allow you to have a pet, and if so, what size?

Once you have completed this application and are accepted as a prospective adopter, the next process is interviewing. The purpose of the personal interview is to determine which dog in the program best suits your needs. Then your references will be checked. Many times, a copy of your lease showing you have permission to have a dog is required. Some groups may even come out to see your home. Your veterinarian might be called (if you already have one), as well as your previous dog's breeder or anyone else you list on the application. You may receive a call from more than one person in the organization during the interview process. This is all done in the interest of finding a dog who suits you, one you will be pleased to have in your home.

The group will begin looking for a dog who would be a good match for you. When a dog is identified, you are contacted and given the pertinent information of why the dog was turned in to rescue, his age, his health, and other items. Ask questions about the dog. Remember, it could take a week, a month, or a couple of months, but placing a rescue dog in the right home is most important, because it is difficult for dogs to adjust to a new home over and over again. Rescue groups want to get it right the first time. Therefore, they go to great effort to make sure the dog you get is the right dog for you.

When you get your call about a prospective dog, you will be given an opportunity to meet the dog. Rescue dogs are found all over the country,

The Fenced Yard

Some rescue groups will place dogs only with people who have fenced yards. Their thought is that with a fenced yard, the dog has a safe place to wander and relieve himself.

But a fenced yard is not necessarily a sign of a good dog owner. Many dogs are placed every year with people who live in apartments or whose yards are not fenced, but who are responsible enough to put a leash on their dog and walk him, both to relieve himself and for exercise.

Don't make the mistake of thinking that a fenced yard will take care of all a dog's needs. Dogs are companions. They want to be with you. They love attention, and usually they are happy to be with you even if you are only watching television or surfing the Internet.

Dogs in yards by themselves can sometimes lead to trouble. They may dig holes and escape. They may develop the bad habit of barking at every noise, which will disturb your neighbors. A dog who spends most of his time alone in a fenced yard will not be happy or well behaved.

so your prospective dog may be in Ohio while you are in Oklahoma. Hopefully, a face-to-face visit is possible. No rescue group will force you to take a dog. If, after you meet the dog and play with him, you have doubts, say so. The important thing is that all parties involved are comfortable with the adoption.

Rescue volunteers get a keen sense of when something just does not seem right. Perhaps it is something that was said during the interview, and sometimes they can never quite put their finger on what the problem is.

The rescue organization, especially the person who fostered the dog and knows the dog, may call you several times during your first month with your new dog. You will also get calls for several months just to make sure the transition is going smoothly. Since the foster volunteer had the dog for awhile, she can answer some of the questions or give you insight into the dog's behavior.

Apartment Dwellers

Dogs of appropriate size and temperament can live happily in apartments, provided they are given sufficient exercise and attention. If you live in an apartment, it's best to search for a toy or small dog to share your home, such as a Maltese, Dachshund, or Pug. Dogs of this size can be easily taken with you when you go out, either in your arms or in a doggy tote bag. Large and giant breeds such as Great Danes and Newfoundlands need lots of room to stretch their legs and won't be able to accompany you on a bus, in a taxi, or on the train the way a small dog in his tote bag can.

No dog will thrive if the family is not home. Dogs left alone too long in apartments can become destructive and chew your rugs and furniture out of frustration or boredom. (Of course, the same is true for dogs left alone in big houses or in fenced yards.) Or, they may try to signal their loneliness by barking, and even small dogs can bark loudly enough to disturb your neighbors. A small dog who can often go with you when you leave home is your best bet.

New Yorkers who live in tall buildings sometimes set up a "potty area" right in the apartment, perhaps in the kitchen or bathroom, so they are not locked into a schedule of taking the dog out every few hours. A new product on the market is the doggy litter box, which is another good tool for apartment dwellers—but it really only works for small dogs.

Basic obedience training is especially important for apartment-dwelling family dogs, since they will require daily on-leash exercise on crowded city streets. Walking a dog who pulls constantly, jumps, and/or routinely barks at other dogs gets old very quickly. Walking the dog becomes an unpleasant burden instead of an enjoyable opportunity to spend time with the family pet. Basic obedience classes are available in cities everywhere, and beginner classes cover the basics you and your dog will need to have a happy urban relationship.

The majority of reputable breeders support breed rescue, and many national breed clubs and local dog clubs contribute financially to rescue efforts for their breed. Many volunteers in local rescue groups are also reputable breeders. One problem rescue organizations are up against, however, is the stigma among some breeders that rescue dogs are bad apples. There may be some, but the rescue workers do an excellent job of weeding out the problem dogs. Perhaps breeders feel there's a sense of competition: "If you adopt a dog from a rescue group, you aren't going to buy one from me." But perhaps the person who got their first dog from rescue will purchase a puppy from a breeder a few years down the road, when they have totally fallen in love with the breed or have more money to spend on a dog, or both. Meanwhile, the dog has a new home, the person has a breed they want, and the breeder will have her sale, all in due time. In the long run, everyone wins.

Over the years, I have had many dogs. My first was a shelter dog, a Beagle-terrier mix named Tippy. She was a sweet dog, but had a mind of her own. Many times, her scenting instincts from her Beagle background would take her down to the neighbors to join in on their picnic. We have had dogs that were purchased from breeders who were a great joy and we have bred our own dogs.

But one thing is different with rescue dogs. They seem to know you want them. They have seen the bad side and have lived in homes where they were not loved—at least, not enough to be kept. After that abandonment, they seem to really appreciate their new home. I have a rescue dog now named Frosty who was abandoned at a shelter at four months of age, at nine months, and again at twelve months. Then he was taken in by someone who gave him no real discipline. This new owner just could not handle Frosty's exuberance. At eighteen months of age, Frosty again was looking for a home. This poor dog has not had an opportunity to unpack his bag and stay anywhere for more than a few months. But he is not crazy. He is a typical happy, fun-loving Weimaraner who has energy to burn. It took him a long time to find someone who understands him. He is just a healthy boy who needs lots of exercise to burn off his energy. In return, he has proven to be a loving friend.

Shelters

The shelter you are most likely to visit is the local one, run either by the town or the Society for the Prevention of Cruelty to Animals (SPCA). Shelters may be kill or no-kill. According to Sue Sternberg, an expert on shelters and the author of *Successful Dog Adoption*, the majority of municipally run facilities are kill shelters. These shelters will take in any animal, regardless of his temperament or circumstances. Because of this open-admission policy, they must put to death some animals to make room for more coming in. Sometimes, dogs who are not considered adoptable at a no-kill shelter will end up at an open-admission facility.

No-kill shelters will not destroy a dog unless the dog is in obvious agony. Most no-kill shelters only take in problem-free dogs that can easily be adopted out to new families, and if this is the policy at the shelter you visit, it's a good place to find a nice dog. But some no-kill shelters do not screen their charges so carefully, and with some dogs, their aggression problems do not show up right away. So a no-kill shelter may have dogs who have been there a long time and are, essentially, unadoptable.

Sternberg has found that the temperament and the breeds of dogs in a shelter vary according to whether the shelter is near a large urban area

This Siberian Husky was too big for the woman to handle, so he is being turned over to an animal shelter. Yet, he might be a perfect pet for another person.

or is in a rural area. Shelters near large cities tend to have more of the fighting or aggressive breeds, plus strays and owner-surrendered dogs. Dogs found in rural shelters are, for the most part, stray farm dogs, lost or stolen hunting dogs, the products of unplanned litters, or dogs bred for a specific job who just aren't good workers. (*Successful Dog Adoption* is an excellent reference and a must-read book for people looking for shelter dogs. It delves deeply into the topic of shelter adoption.)

The aggressive dogs found in the city shelters are breeds such as the Rottweiler, Pit Bull, and Chow Chow. These dogs are sometimes used by gangs for dog fighting competitions or by businesses as guard dogs. It is these dogs who usually end up at shelters, because rescue groups cannot risk taking these dogs in. These dogs cannot be rehabilitated into pets after they have spent their entire life training to fight to survive. These dogs may be overly sensitive to innocent motions—even normal running, yelling, and playing may seem threatening to them.

It's important to keep in mind, however, that well-bred and well-socialized dogs of any breed, including Pit Bulls, can be loving pets. There are many examples of such dogs being adopted and turning into great family dogs, exhibiting no problems at all. But since these dogs show up at the shelter with no information about their former lives, and they may be the product of poor breeding and trained for illegal activities, you need to do your homework before adopting one.

The adoption process with some shelters is very similar to that of rescue groups. There will be applications and other paperwork, interviews, and visits. The interview process, again, asks questions about your background with pets, lifestyle, and family to assist you in making a good match. Most shelters want you to be prescreened before allowing you to see the animals. However, some will allow you to see the various dogs available for adoption. Many times, shelters that allow you in right off the street do not have a formal adoption policy or screening. Be careful of situations like this.

Ask the shelter personnel what their policy is on temperament testing, evaluating the animals, and returning a dog. Some shelters do extensive temperament testing, while others may tell you only what they have seen the dog do inside his cage. Ask what kind of help you can expect to make this a smooth transfer.

The Anti-Cruelty Society of Chicago is one of the largest shelters in the country and is highly regarded. It receives approximately 15,000 animals a year. The animals that are brought in are either stray, abandoned, or surrendered by their owners. They are carefully observed, and this information, along with the information from the surrendering party, becomes part of the dog's file. The staff is trained to help people make an informed choice.

The requirements at the Anti-Cruelty Society to adopt a dog are:

You must be 18 years of age.

You must provide photo identification with your current address.

You must provide the landlord's telephone number.

You must provide the current lease that shows animals are allowed.

Shelter personnel do verification checks with everyone living in the house to make sure all are in agreement before an animal is released to the family's care. This shelter has special programs available to adopters, such as a behavior hotline, training classes, and programs for senior citizens. They also provide a low-income clinic, a mobile veterinary clinic, and a spay/neuter clinic.

After the paperwork is completed, it's time to see the dogs. Depending on how the shelter area is configured, adoptable dogs may be housed in one area while the more aggressive dogs are kept in another part of the facility. Many times, depending on space and funds, they are intermixed. It is very important when looking at the dogs to watch their body language. Obviously, those who are snarling and showing their teeth are giving you a hint of what is ahead. Unfortunately, trying to read canine body language is not always easy, especially if the dogs are excited by the sight of people unfamiliar to them.

Some problems are very fixable through training, such as jumping, pulling, and housesoiling. Other problems, such as growling, snarling, and biting, are not fixable, but are traits in that dog, whether bred into him or environmental in nature. Unfortunately, some shelters allow people to adopt known aggressive dogs. And aggressive dogs may not show signs of their real temperament until some stress pushes the situation.

As you go into the kennel in a shelter, watch for dogs who exhibit signs of aggression. This includes not looking relaxed, a tucked or stiff tail, frozen in one position, showing the whites of their eyes, eyes dilated, panting, agitation, and lowering the head. An aggressive dog will growl to warn you to go away, snarl to show his teeth, and try to nip. Walk away from this dog!

Another temperament fault to watch for in dogs is fearfulness. Dogs may show fear of things in their environment or of people. Environmental

Dogs like this Collie give us an excuse to get out and meet people.

triggers might include a loud noise, storms, or objects that are unfamiliar to the dog. You can help a fearful dog by encouraging him to slowly investigate the object or noise, so he learns that it will not hurt him. This will help him build confidence. Regular training will also help a fearful dog become more confident.

Dogs who are fearful of people pose a more serious problem. Although such a dog may bond with people in his new home, he will have problems out in public, which could cause him to growl and possibly bite. He may be just fine at home, but living with a fearful-aggressive dog is like walking on eggshells. One little situation can set him off. A dog who is fearful of strangers can develop into what is called a *fear biter*. These are dogs who will bite if they feel threatened or trapped.

When you see a dog who is of interest to you, ask if the dog has been temperament tested and ask to review his records. Ask to take the dog out and walk him around. Does he allow you to pet him? Does he snuggle up to you or is he aloof? Bring a toy and see how he plays with it. When you walk near the dog, does he try to protect the toy? Does his tail wag? Does the dog look up at you? Watch his eyes: Are they dilated? Do you see the whites of the eyes? Is the dog relaxed or does he always have an eye on you?

Pet Supply Stores

Another opportunity to look at adoptable animals is through programs sponsored by Petsmart and Petco. Both organizations sponsor adoption centers in which animals from various local humane organizations are brought in for the public to see.

According to Petsmart, each year between 10 and 15 million pets are abandoned, and half are put to death because homes cannot be found for them. Petsmart partners with local adoption groups and provides supplies to them. All adoption fees derived from in-store adoptions stay with the adoption group. Petsmart Charities, a nonprofit organization, has found homes for 1.5 million homeless pets since 1992. In addition, this organization has given more than $24 million to local humane agencies. It provides grants to nonprofit organizations, governmental animal control agencies, and educational institutions. In addition, they provide funding for adoption programs and spay/neuter services.

The Petco Foundation was established in 1999 to work hands-on with animal welfare organizations throughout the country. The foundation promotes charitable, educational, and philanthropic activities to assist companion animals everywhere. Petco found homes for 11,527 orphaned animals during its Adoption Days over a two-day period, an achievement of which they are justly proud.

Petco raised $1.1 million in its first year through a variety of programs, such as the Tree of Hope, Spring a Pet, Round Up, National Pet Adoption Days, and the Disaster Relief Fund. It granted funds to more than 1,200 animal welfare groups. The Petco Foundation Disaster Relief Fund granted more than $500,000 to various groups that participated in search and rescue and housed animals abandoned due to the tragic events of September 11, 2001.

Pet Shops

Pet shops are not the same as pet supply stores. Pet supply stores offer a convenient source for a large selection of food, toys, grooming items, and equipment. Pet shops sell pets. Like all retail businesses, they make their profit by keeping costs down and selling their products at the market rate. Puppies from responsible breeders may cost anywhere from $300 to $2,000 or more, depending on the breed and the background of the dog. Obviously, a pet shop cannot make any profit if it pays the going rate to a reputable breeder for these dogs. So to keep costs down and profits up, pet shops turn to suppliers who will charge them less for their dogs: puppy mills, brokers, and backyard breeders.

Some pet shops belong to professional associations and subscribe to a professional code of conduct that requires them to maintain minimum standards of cleanliness, health, and humane care for the animals they sell. They also offer health guarantees. Some do not.

A child playing with her pal.

There is no requirement to belong to any professional association to sell puppies, although states and municipalities do regulate minimum standards of care for the sale of livestock. They may also require that a shop offer certain health guarantees. Facilities are not frequently inspected, however, and these laws are not rigorously enforced.

If the store you buy your puppy from does not subscribe to a professional code of conduct, the puppy you buy may be unvaccinated, may have worms or other parasites, and may be susceptible to other health problems. When the pups are treated, it may be with medications onsite without the supervision of a veterinarian. Puppies who do not appear ill may harbor viruses that are passed on to other puppies in the store. The puppy you are interested in may seem healthy, and health problems may not show up until after you get him home. Unless the puppy is obviously sick, there really is no way of knowing.

It is all too true that there are pet store owners out there who know that for many people, the minute they pay for and cuddle a puppy, he becomes theirs for life. If the pup becomes ill, the store owner is going to offer a replacement, but it is already too late because the new owners love *this* puppy and don't want to exchange him for another one.

Look-Alike Puppies

When Diane Taylor was breeding Shetland Sheepdogs, her vet asked her if she would speak to a woman who had a Sheltie puppy she had bought from a pet store who was now having a problem. This lady had done all the right research to pick this breed. She had two kids, one nine and one going on eleven. She decided a Sheltie would be a good dog for them because it would not overpower the kids

After six months, she began to wonder what was wrong because the puppy kept growing and growing and growing. She brought the dog for Taylor to see, without the kids, because she didn't want them to be upset if the breeder thought there was something wrong. The dog jumped out of the car, Taylor took one look and asked, "How is this dog working out?"

"Absolutely marvelous!" was the reply. The woman was very happy. She said the dog got along with her children and she'd had no problems training her. The dog was healthy, she had been taking her in for shots and had done everything right. She showed Taylor the AKC papers and the pedigree. She said, "The dog is a whole lot bigger than we expected, after our research. Other than that, she is no problem whatsoever."

Pet shop puppies may also be very healthy—especially if the pet shop owner is a member of a professional organization and takes its code of conduct seriously. However, these puppies are spending some very crucial weeks in their behavioral development in an environment that is not conducive to proper socialization. At a time when responsible breeders are exposing their puppies to a wide variety of people and situations under controlled circumstances so the puppies do not grow up frightened of men, hats, or lawn mowers, pet store puppies are in cages or in the front window of a shop, either alone or with a gang of other puppies, being stared at, poked at, and startled. This is not the best way to develop a happy, friendly, confident pet.

Taylor replied, "That's good, because what you've got here is not a Sheltie. What you've got is a Smooth Collie."

There's a big difference! This dog, at eight months old, was about twenty-three inches tall at the shoulder. Shelties are usually about twelve inches at the shoulder. Over fifteen inches is a disqualification, according to the breed standard.

When the woman went back to the pet shop, she found out that the teenage kids who worked there did not know the difference. This Collie was eight weeks old when she came in, and the kids put her in the same cage with the Sheltie puppies, who were twelve weeks old. They all looked alike to them. They gave her registration papers and a pedigree for a Sheltie puppy, too, so clearly their record-keeping left a lot to be desired.

The first thing they said at the pet store was, "Give the dog back." But she didn't want to do that because she and her family loved the dog. The story ends happily because the vet and Taylor wrote out affidavits about the breed, and, upon presentation of a spay certificate, the store refunded her purchase price (she had paid an exorbitant amount—much more than Taylor charged for real Sheltie puppies!). Plus, she kept the dog.

During this time, responsible breeders start housetraining their puppies, and also begin some basic training. But neither of these things will happen in a pet shop. In fact, pet shop puppies can be particularly difficult to house train. That's because puppies have a natural instinct to soil away from where they play and sleep. Responsible breeders take advantage of this instinct to begin to teach puppies to soil only in a particular place, rather than wherever they happen to be standing when they feel the urge to go. But puppies in cages and shop windows lined with shredded paper have no choice but to soil where they are. Soon, their natural inclination not to do so disappears.

The Case of the Purloined Pedigree

The pedigree that came with a dog I rescued several years ago (the dog was originally purchased through a pet store) said that the sire was a "German import" and a dual champion. Since I competed against this exact sire twenty-five years ago and am friends with the owner, I knew better. There was no way that dog was a German import, and he was not the sire of those puppies either, because this particular dog was never used for breeding. In fact, this dog died many years before the AKC authorized the use of frozen semen for breeding. Thus, this pedigree was stolen and the true heritage of the puppy will never be known. If the puppy was later used for breeding, his paperwork would invalidate the pedigrees of all his progeny. I forwarded the AKC paperwork to the owners of the supposed "German import" sire so that they could take the appropriate legal action. The entire litter's registration was canceled and the breeder was fined and suspended. With today's technology, the AKC and UKC are using DNA testing to determine parentage, and such frauds are becoming easier to detect.

Pet shop puppies, if purebred, usually come with registration papers—either from the AKC or the United Kennel Club (UKC). Without these papers, there is no guarantee that the puppy is the breed he is represented to be. However, the integrity of any registration system relies on the honesty of all the participants. Some pet shops—and some unethical breeders—do fudge the paperwork. Responsible breeders (and honest pet shops) will not do this, because they risk having their registration privileges revoked by the AKC—something that really matters to a reputable breeder, who is competing with her dogs. In addition, to get around the strict requirements of AKC registration, some pet shops have formed their own registries with names like American Kennel Association, which are nothing more than names on a fancy certificate.

Some pet shops and dishonest breeders will exploit a puppy whose appearance may have a disqualifying fault, saying that he is a rare and valuable animal, such as a blue-eyed Whippet, a multicolored Poodle, a blue Weimaraner, or an Irish Setter with white splashes. These faults are rare for the breed because they are considered undesirable in the breed. Responsible breeders do not intentionally breed for a disqualifying fault. Some faults that seem innocent enough, such as coat color, may also be linked to certain genetic defects that can cause health problems.

When you go to a pet shop to buy a puppy, generally they will make sure you have enough money to buy the dog. They may or may not give you any advice on what to feed him or how to care for him. They will not help you pick a puppy that best suits your family and your lifestyle. They will not match the temperament of the puppy to your personality. They will not be available for follow-up questions weeks, months, and even years later. They will not take the puppy back if you can't keep him.

For all these reasons, responsible breeders do not sell their puppies through pet shops. Pet shops may tell you they get their puppies from local breeders, but anyone who breeds dogs in your state may be called a local breeder. That's not the same as a responsible breeder. So where do pet shop puppies come from?

One place is puppy brokers. Brokers are middlemen: They buy up available puppies and sell them to pet shops, auctions, and other outlets. Generally, brokers get their puppies from puppy mills and backyard breeders. Pet shops may also do business directly with these sources.

Puppy Mills

Puppy mills are farms that raise puppies in large quantities, specifically for pet shops and dog auctions. These farms give no consideration for the temperament, heredity, or health problems of their dogs, much less the soundness and breed type specified by the breed standard. As long as two dogs are purebred, they will be bred over and over again.

Some (although not all) puppy mills keep their dogs in very unsanitary, inhumane conditions. The puppies may be confined in very small crates or pens, may not be fed the optimum diet for breeding animals, and may be kept in areas where it is not clean and not safe. Some puppy mills provide regular veterinary care; some do not. Some dogs suffer greatly under conditions of ill health and ill care. Some are kept in clean, bright pens with proper health care. But in most cases, dogs in puppy mills are of inferior breeding stock and are not kept as companion animals.

Conscientious breeding produces healthy and beautiful dogs like Zippy, who is owned and trained by the author. (UACH Ch. Mehagian's Zip-A-Dee-Doo-Dah, CD, SH, AXP, OAJ, OA, OJP, CGC, VC)

Females are bred frequently—sometimes at every heat cycle—and are confined with their litters to wire pens or other small enclosures. Males are kept separately and are used exclusively for breeding. These farms have only a few males, who are used to breed a large number of females, and dogs are often interbred (bred to close relatives) over several generations, so that the farm can keep the minimum number of dogs and produce the maximum number of puppies. A pedigree from a puppy mill dog will often contain the same few names in several generations. Once the female becomes too old or too ill to breed, she is usually destroyed. Puppies are often removed from their mothers at four to five weeks of age and in some cases are barely weaned. This is so they will be available at the pet shop while they are still young enough to be on display for several weeks. These puppies have received very little human contact and therefore are not properly socialized.

Puppies go through a series of growth development stages and must remain with their mothers to learn the various attributes of becoming a good dog (for more on puppy development stages, see chapter 6). Up to the age of eight weeks, a puppy learns many things from his mother and siblings; for example, that he should be submissive to older, bigger animals, like his mother; and that if he plays too hard and bites one of his siblings, they will bite back and hurt *him*. He learns to keep his sleeping area clean and to move far away to relieve himself. If puppies are removed during this stage, they may become overly noisy and have discipline problems. They have not had time to learn the important things a puppy needs to know.

Buying a puppy from a pet shop creates a demand for puppies raised under these conditions. Pet shops keep puppy mills in business. And people keep pet shops in business.

Backyard Breeders

The other place pet shops get their puppies from are backyard breeders who cannot place all their puppies in homes. Backyard breeders are casual breeders who may be familiar with their own dog but not with the specifics of the breed in general. They're the kind of people who say, "Let's breed Fifi so she experiences the joy of motherhood," or "We want our children to experience the miracle of birth," or "Let's make a couple bucks by breeding dogs," or "Fifi is so sweet that we'd like to have some puppies from her."

Since these breeders are usually not knowledgeable about the health or hereditary problems associated with the breed, they do not test for them to make sure they are not passing along genetic problems that will arise later, such as hip dysplasia or blindness. They do not carefully choose Fifi's mate—often, he's the only dog in the neighborhood who happens to be the same breed as Fifi—and are not concerned with improving the breed by breeding away from faults and flaws or any of the other considerations that go into a careful breeding program.

These breeders usually do not belong to any clubs, nor are they active in the sport. The quality of their dogs has not been proven by the rigors of competition. They do not take the time to learn about genetics and animal husbandry. Many times, they have a hard time finding homes for all the puppies and turn to pet shops to help place them.

These dogs are usually socialized with the breeder's family and kids, so you're less likely to see the behavioral problems associated with dogs from puppy mills. However, these dogs have not been bred with the same thought and care as a dog from a responsible breeder. They may or may not be healthy and sound. There is really no way of knowing.

Newspapers and Specialty Magazines

Specialty magazines cover every sport in the dog world. There are family-oriented magazines such as *DogWorld* and *Dog Fancy*. Most of the breeders in these magazines are not considered backyard breeders or puppy mills. However, you still need to use the information you have learned to make sure you are dealing with an honest and legitimate breeder.

If you are looking for a sporting dog, there are many sporting dog magazines that carry breeder ads. *Bloodlines* is the UKC's magazine. *Front and Finish* is a publication directed toward obedience enthusiasts. *Field and Stream* and *Gun Dog* are magazines specializing in hunting breeds. For herding breeds, there's *National Stockdog Magazine*.

Although you can find good dogs through newspaper advertisements, you must be careful. Remember, pet shops, puppy mills, and backyard breeders advertise in the newspaper, as do reputable breeders. You need to determine whether the person you are talking with is a legitimate breeder.

Here are five examples of advertisements taken from the newspaper in my area. By looking at them closely, you can figure out which of these have been placed by responsible breeders.

1. "Weimaraner pups, AKC, OFA, dual champions, both lines, dam & sire. Ready, January 13."

2. "Weimaraner pups, AKC. Exc. Hunters & pets. No white spots, $350."

3. "Weimaraner pups, beautiful pups, AKC 6 weeks. Rare 'blue' and 'fawn.'"

4. "Weimaraner pups, exe. Hunters and pets. 6 weeks. Will deliver."

5. "Puppies, Huskies, Yorkies, Pugs, Rotts large selection, V/MC accepted."

Without enough information about the breed, all of these newspaper advertisements might look inviting. Three say the dogs are AKC registered.

That sounds reputable, but the AKC is only a registry and does not control which dogs breeders use in their breeding programs or the quality of the dogs used. As long as both parents are registered purebred animals, the offspring can also be registered. So just because the puppies are AKC registered does not mean that they are of good quality. What do the phrases "no white spots," "blue and fawn," "OFA," and "dual champions" mean? This is the additional information the breeder uses to catch your eye, and it can tell you a lot.

Advertisement 1 is from a responsible breeder. The puppies' parents have been certified by the OFA to be clear of hip dysplasia, a congenital and crippling joint disease. OFA certification is not cheap, so this breeder has clearly put some effort into choosing the dogs for this mating. She must also compete with her dogs, because she says they are dual champions. Dual champions are dogs who have earned the necessary qualifying wins to be called Champions in two different areas of competition. Is this good? You bet! The ideal is when the championships are in conformation (the structure and appearance of the dog) and in the work they were bred to do (which, with the Weimaraner, means hunting).

Advertisement 2 is from a backyard breeder. She knows that white spots, if properly placed, are acceptable but that a solid dog is preferable. This means she has read the Weimaraner standard. This advertiser does not say whether she has checked the dog's hips or whether she competes with the dogs. When you answer such an ad, be sure to ask about these things, as well as why she breeds, her experience, what she is doing about health concerns in the breed, and whether she offers a guarantee on these puppies.

Advertisement 3 is from another backyard breeder. This breeder is advertising a disqualifying fault—blue—as a "rare" dog and may even be selling it at premium price. You must read the Weimaraner standard to know this (it's available online at the AKC Web site, www.akc.org). Yes, blue is a rare color, but that's because it is a disqualification in the breed standard and reputable breeders do not intentionally breed for this color. A blue dog should not be used for breeding. This advertiser also indicates that she would be willing to sell the puppies before the recommended (and usually mandated by state law) minimum age of eight weeks. Your best course of action is not to call this advertiser.

Advertisement 4 seems to be from a puppy wholesaler. She is selling the puppies too young and is willing to bring them to your home—which means you will not be screened as a buyer. It's very likely that little attention, if any, was given to the genetic and health issues of the breed. The only thing I can say is *run!*

Advertisement 5 should be easily recognized as from a pet shop, since reputable breeders generally raise only one or two breeds. Also, the fact that this advertiser takes Visa and MasterCard indicates that she is a business and deals in a high volume of puppies (I haven't heard of any reputable breeders who take Visa or MasterCard as payment), in which case the puppies are unlikely to have received the individual attention required for good socialization.

6

The Breeder and You

Once you have analyzed the pros and cons of the breed you want and feel comfortable with your decision, it is time to interview breeders. By now you should be familiar with the following information on the breed of your choice:

- The breed's history and original purpose, which are part of what determines its temperament
- The time and commitment the breed will require for exercise and grooming
- The health and genetic problems of the breed
- About what it will cost to own the breed (including vet care, feeding, and grooming)
- The names of local and national breeders and the breed rescue organization (obtained from the national breed club, see appendix B)

Now it's time to find a reputable breeder. Interview several breeders and work with one you feel comfortable with, not just the first person who has puppies at that moment. Don't be afraid to ask questions. She may tell you that her dogs are the best in the area, but do not hesitate to question her further about her background, experience, goals in breeding, and her dogs. A reputable breeder has nothing to hide and will be very happy to discuss these things with you. It is the unethical and irresponsible breeder who may take offense at your line of questioning. Does the breeder speak negatively of her peers? Steer clear of people like this; those breeders she speaks poorly of are often her biggest rivals in competition. By asking a variety of questions, you should be able to get an idea of whether this is an ethical, responsible breeder or just a good salesperson.

When speaking with a breeder, be prepared to answer a lot of questions, as well. After all, she is entrusting an animal's care to you. Most breeders will ask about the age of your children and your past experience with dogs, because a reputable breeder would not want to give you a puppy who is not right for you.

What makes a good breeder? In my opinion it is a person who:

- Cares about her dogs and the breed
- Is honest about the quality of her dogs
- Has medical certifications for her breeding animals so she knows they do not have certain inherited health problems, and will readily show you the certifications upon request
- Carefully screens potential homes and places puppies appropriately for their safety and well-being
- Is active in the breed and informed about what is happening in the breed and the world of dogs
- Is available to her puppy owners to consult and answer questions
- Encourages you to learn about the breed through training, club activities, and competition

Finding a Good Breeder

Comparing the story of Marge Mehagian, a responsible breeder (see the box on page 86), with the story of another breeder whose ethics are questionable (see the box on page 88) illustrates the importance of doing your homework to find a good breeder.

Leila Downen of Diablesse Kennel with her Brussels Griffons.

It is up to you to ask questions, based on what you have learned and your personal experience, to find a good breeder. The person you choose could be a valuable asset throughout your dog's life. In the pages that follow, I list a number of questions you should ask every breeder before you decide to do business with her. Take notes that you can use to compare one breeder to another.

The Right Breeder

Marge Mehagian of Mehagian Vizslas has been involved in her breed for forty years. Her dogs compete in conformation, field trials, obedience, and other sporting events. She has been a member of the Vizsla Club of America for thirty-eight years and has served on the board of directors since 1977 as director and currently as vice president. She is a founding member of the Rio Salado Vizsla Club in Arizona, serving that club in many capacities, including president. She is the owner of DC AFC 2xNFC NAFC Mehagian's Peppy Paloma, HOF, a dog who won several national championships and has been inducted into the Vizsla Club of America's Hall of Fame. Her first dog, Ch. Sandor Barat, HOF, has been recognized as a Top Producer and is also in the Hall of Fame.

"It is important for a breeder to be involved in a variety of activities to showcase her dogs," says Mehagian. "Competing against other dogs validates her breeding program. Anyone can breed dogs by putting two dogs together, and that is what backyard breeders and puppy mills do. It is the responsible breeder who competes with her dogs and proves her dogs' quality."

When working with families looking for dogs, "I invite them to my home so we get a chance to know each other," she says. "To me, this is a hobby. My first concern is placing a puppy in a home that will be compatible for all involved. We discuss their lifestyle, family commitments, and the importance of spending time with the dog so that the dog is properly socialized."

She looks for the level of discipline that exists between the parents and children—will the children follow the parents' instructions about how to interact with and care for the dog? Her interview process also gives her an idea of how high-energy a puppy the family should get. "I try to match a puppy that I believe will be successful for them," she says.

One of the most important parts of Mehagian's puppy sales contract addresses the issue of what happens if the family cannot keep the dog. "I will always take my dogs back," she says. "My contract states that the buyer cannot sell or dispose of the animal without my consent. I want to know where my puppies go."

She encourages people to attend training classes, some of which she teaches in her backyard. "We have a great club because so many people come out and train and enjoy working with their dog. It is contagious."

"Sometimes during the interview process you get this gut feeling that perhaps an addition of a puppy into a family, for whatever reason, is not a good idea. I know it's hard at times, but sometimes I have to say to someone 'No, not now.' Responsible breeders keep the welfare of all involved in mind—the prospective family and the puppy."

Marge Mehagian, a dedicated Vizsla breeder.

The Wrong Breeder

Diane's son wanted a dog. She helped him do some research and had finally narrowed their choice to one breed. Through the newspaper, Diane found someone who had puppies for sale. That evening, Diane took her son to the breeder's home. The puppies they saw seemed lethargic and thin. They were small, but the breeder insisted that they were twelve weeks old. Diane felt uneasy because the breeder was not willing to answer all her questions. The price, $1,000, was a lot more than other breeders had asked. But Diane was anxious to get a puppy for her son, so she paid, signed a contract, and took the puppy.

The next morning, the puppy was vomiting and not eating or drinking. Diane took the dog to the vet and was shocked when he told her that the puppy was no more than seven weeks old. The vet also believed the puppy had a serious health problem. She called the breeder and left a message. It was not returned.

The puppy became ill again, necessitating more trips to the emergency clinic. Medical expenses rose and so did telephone bills, but the breeder never returned her calls.

Finally, surgery confirmed the existence of liver shunts—abnormal veins that allow blood for the intestines to bypass the liver. Sometimes, these can be corrected with surgery, but in this case the surgeon discovered the shunts were too numerous to repair. Finally, Diane reached the breeder, who was unsympathetic and told her to return the puppy. But after investing so much financially and emotionally, Diane could not bear to send the puppy back.

Then Diane faced another setback: The puppy could no longer swallow his food. Again, she took him to the veterinarian. Again surgery was performed. This time the diagnosis was a right aorta arch that was strangulating the puppy's esophagus. The surgeon tried to repair this defect but, unfortunately, the puppy died on the operating table.

Diane sent a certified letter to the breeder. It went unanswered. Finally, the only way to get any response from the breeder was through a lawsuit. Diane sued the breeder for misrepresenting the age of the puppy and his health condition. Diane won her case and received her purchase money back and half of her medical expenses. But did Diane really win? She had wanted a healthy puppy she and her son could love. Instead, they were left with months of emotional upheaval, ending in heartbreak.

How Old Are the Puppies and at What Age Can They Go to Their New Homes?

Puppies should stay with their mother and siblings until eight weeks of age, and many state laws require that puppies not be sold before that age. This is not an arbitrary decision, but is based on fifty years of research by animal behaviorists. Studies have shown that puppies go through mental development phases and experiences each week that help prepare them for adulthood and make them well-balanced animals. These critical periods in a puppy's life begin at birth and extend through the maturity of the dog. Dr. Clarence Pfaffenberger, one of the pioneering researchers in canine behavior, divides these periods as follows.

The *neonatal period* begins at birth and continues for thirteen days. During this time, puppies require food and warmth and become aware of sounds, smells, and direct contact. The *transition period* runs from day thirteen to day twenty-one. This is the age at which the eyes and ears open and the puppies begin seeing and hearing things. They start to respond to smells, tastes, and objects. The *awareness period* begins about twenty-one days of age and runs to twenty-three days. It is an opportune time to introduce new floor surfaces and new textures to puppies, but for very short periods of time. Puppies receiving mild stresses during the first five weeks of their lives are able to handle stress better and learn more quickly later in life.

The *canine socialization period* overlaps a bit with the awareness period, running from twenty-one days to forty-nine days. (Please note that forty-nine days is seven weeks.) During this period, the puppy must be kept with his littermates and his mother. He will learn how to be submissive to his mother and how to respond to the play of his littermates. If he is removed from the litter during this period, he may become overly bossy or fearful and have discipline problems. Five weeks of age is an excellent time for the breeder to start the litter on mini–obedience lessons and to introduce them to new people.

Puppy temperament testing is done on day 49 or after, since the brain waves of the puppy are now as developed as those of an adult dog. Tests on puppies who have been properly socialized and have not experienced any traumatic episodes should be reliable in determining which puppies will excel as pets and competitors. Many breeders use these tests to help place puppies in homes. Puppies can start going home at this age, but their socialization to humans, situations, and objects must continue for many more weeks.

There are other developmental periods as well. The Seniority Classification Period starts at twelve to sixteen weeks, when a puppy starts losing his baby teeth. This is when a puppy is testing his place in your family group. It is especially important that he be discouraged from nipping and playing games such as tug-of-war during this period. The next period is the Flight Instinct Period, which takes place from four to eight months. The puppy starts to test his wings at this time, and may not come when called. Pfaffenberger suggests just keeping your puppy on the leash until this period passes.

Pfaffenberger also found that there are several Fear Impact Periods that can affect puppies. The first of these periods can occur from eight to ten weeks of age. The experiences a pup has at this age, such as trips to the veterinarian, can affect his attitude for his entire life. The second Fear Impact Period, is from six to fourteen months, and can even extend into the maturity. During this period, the puppy fears new situations. Pfaffenberger suggests helping your puppy work his way through this period by using praise, encouragement, and lots of treats for reassurance. The last fear period is when a dog is a young adult, from eighteen to twenty-four months. He may show a rise in his level of aggression, become protective and territorial, and attempt to dominate you. (To learn more about this topic, I recommend *How to Raise a Puppy You Can Live With* by Clarice Rutherford and Dr. David Neil, and Clarence Pfaffenberger's landmark work, *The New Knowledge of Dog Behavior*.)

Has the Puppy Been Temperament Tested?

Not all puppies of the same breed are alike, not even puppies of the same litter. Some puppies will be very easy to get along with, while others will test the patience of the entire household. Many breeders use temperament tests as a tool in placing dogs in their permanent homes. There are many types of puppy temperament tests; the one I use was developed in 1979 to help breeders, trainers, and puppy buyers decide which pups are best suited for the show ring, field sports, service dog work such as guide dogs, and family pets. At forty-nine days or older, puppies are individually put through a battery of tests that include social attractions, following humans, restraint, social dominance, elevated dominance, retrieving, and touch, sound, and sight sensitivity.

There are no right or wrong answers to these tests. They just give the breeder an idea of what kind of dog a puppy will turn out to be. People who are experienced in performing these tests can give you a good idea of the personality of each puppy in a litter, to help determine which one, if any, would be a good fit with your family.

The "social attraction" test gives the tester an idea of how much the puppy is attracted to people. Dogs who have a high level of social attraction do well around people and are comfortable in a human setting. The "following" test measures the puppy's willingness to follow human leadership. A dog who is willing to follow is more likely to look to you for leadership.

Knowing the puppy's temperament is essential to building a lasting relationship with your dog.

In the "restraint" test, the breeder gently places the puppy on his back to see how much he struggles. This will give the tester an idea of the pup's dominance level. A puppy who struggles a lot will want to have a say in who dominates the house. The "social dominance" test looks at how willing the puppy is to accept human dominance by seeing if he takes correction well. The "elevation dominance" test looks at how accepting the puppy is when he is in a position where he has no control. A dog who does not accept these kinds of situations may be digging in his crate or tunneling under your fence.

The "retrieving" test gives some idea of whether a puppy will be easy to train. It has been shown that a puppy who retrieves takes well to training. However, not every pup is interested in retrieving, and that does not mean he is untrainable.

The "touch sensitivity" test lets the tester know how sensitive the puppy is to touch. The area between the toes is pinched, starting from a light pinch to a point when the puppy first shows signs of a struggle. The sound sensitivity test is used to check for shyness to noise. Dogs who are very sensitive to touch and sound may be nervous or shy, and are probably not the best choice for a family with children.

The "chase instinct" test is used to see if the puppy will chase a moving object and helps to show boldness. The stability test shows the degree of reasonable response to a strange object. This is especially important in dogs who are destined for a career in canine sports, because they are always going to new places and meeting new dogs and people.

Puppies are also watched while they play with their littermates to determine their energy level. If you have small children, you do not need a high-energy dog knocking them over.

What Shots Has the Puppy Had and What Does He Need?

There are several batteries of vaccinations that must be given to puppies. Most puppies receive their first shots at five to six weeks of age, with boosters at about seven to eight weeks. Usually, combination injections are given, with one shot containing the vaccines against distemper, hepatitis, corona virus, parainfluenza, and adenovirus. However, some breeds are extremely sensitive to certain components of these vaccines. In such cases, vaccinations need to be broken down into single shots over a longer period of time.

Loyalty Matters

When you find a breeder you are comfortable with, stick with her. Some people shop from breeder to breeder, leave a deposit on a puppy with one person, then decide to do business with another when they find a litter that will be available earlier. When the first breeder calls to say the puppy is ready to go home, she finds out that the buyer already has a puppy from another breeder. This is completely unfair to the first breeder.

If you do this, don't expect to get your deposit back. The first breeder has probably turned away other prospective puppy purchasers, thinking the litter is fully reserved. Generally, deposits are nonrefundable unless the breeder cannot supply you with a puppy or if you wanted a puppy of a certain sex and there were none available.

You should ask the breeder and check with the national breed club to see if there are concerns about using an all-in-one shot. If the national club recommends breaking up the shots, do it. Your veterinarian may see no reason for doing so and may try to talk you into the all-in-one method because the separate shots must be specially ordered. Remember that breeders know the individual health quirks of their breed better than veterinarians; the experience of breeders has fueled many health alerts and subsequent changes in what veterinarians recommend.

If a breeder tells you they have given the puppies "the usual shots" but can't say what the shots are, run. Good breeders know exactly what they have given their puppies and when. If a breeder tells you they have not vaccinated the pups at all, for any reason, run faster.

The breeder should give you the dates and types of shots administered. Puppies are often less active for a day or so after receiving vaccinations, so keep that in mind when you visit them.

Also ask whether the puppies have been wormed. Puppies can get parasites from their mother, so the breeder should have had the puppies tested and, if necessary, treated. You should also be given a complete health history when you take the puppy home, which should include a schedule of future vaccines and the dates they should be done.

Is This Your First Litter?

The experience of the breeder is important. However, the answer to this question should be evaluated in light of the questions that follow. Most responsible breeders have waited a couple of years, during which they compete and learn about the sport and the breed, before having a litter. A first-time breeder may be taking that next step forward by breeding a promising dog.

On the other hand, someone who tells you they have bred dozens of litters might be trying to make a buck by breeding her dog season after season to her friend's dog. Such a person does not do the health certifications necessary to make sure the dogs used for breeding are free from inherited problems.

Look for a breeder who shows a real commitment to improving the breed, whether it is her first litter or her twentieth.

Look to experienced breeders when choosing a dog.

This breeder's family includes children and English Cocker Spaniels.

How Long Have You Been Involved in This Breed?

Did the breeder just get her first dog and have a litter, hoping to recoup the cost of the dog by selling the puppies? This is not a person you want to buy a puppy from. A good breeder studies the breed standard and gets to know the dogs in the breed and what makes them special, and the various bloodlines, long before she breeds a single litter. She has tested her dogs in competition and has won awards. And all that takes time.

Are You a Member of the Local or National Breed Club?

Belonging to a breed club enables a breeder to learn more about their breed, by attending shows and educational events and by spending time with more experienced breeders. Many clubs sponsor seminars on everything from handling in competition to the many health concerns breeders face. National events give breeders an opportunity to see dogs from various parts of the country. Club events also enable people to get together to discuss pertinent breed issues.

A Commitment to the Breed

Kathy and Jeff Engelsman, of JNEK Vizslas, progressed from owning to breeding to judging these Hungarian hunting dogs. They started their competitive work in AKC hunt tests and field trials in 1994. Looking back to when they first started training dogs, Kathy says, "Although I had never trained a dog before, I did train an ex-racehorse to be the Illinois Hunter/Jumper State Champion, and applied that knowledge to our dogs. It was very challenging, to say the least, but very rewarding to see the dog run out to a tree line and lock up on point—seeing his natural ability at work." Kathy and Jeff have several other dogs with Junior Hunter titles, and did the difficult work of earning the Master Hunter title with one dog and Senior Hunter with another. They encourage their puppy owners to become involved in the sport.

They became interested in conformation after attending a seminar I put on for the local Vizsla club about how to successfully train and show a dog. "Competing in field and conformation events cemented the reason for how important it is to have proper structure and natural hunting ability," says Jeff.

As a result of the experience gained in both those areas, their breeding program is very successful. "When we started our breeding program, Jeff and I looked at pedigrees to see what we felt might be a good match," says Kathy. "We liked a certain style and did line breeding to strengthen those features." To date, they have produced several Registry of Merit Dogs, Top Producers, multiple champions, field-pointed dogs, and BIS BISS Ch. JNEK's King Ralph, JH.

As you can see, it is important to work with breeders who have experience. They have learned what best fits into their program and compliments their breeding animals.

It is good to find out how long the breeder has been a member of a club and how active she has been. Someone can be a member of a club for twenty years and never attend events, participate in activities, or learn anything about the breed. People who are actively working on committees and at events have a better idea of how the dogs are expected to look and perform.

What Activities Do You and Your Dogs Compete In?

Between the AKC, the UKC, the Canadian Kennel Club (CKC), national breed clubs, and the various other organizations sponsoring canine sporting events, there is no shortage of ways to compete with a dog. How does the breeder participate with her dogs? Is she involved in one or more of the following sports (not every breed may participate in every sport listed):

Agility	Flyball
Breed Proficiency Tests	Herding
Canine Freestyle	Hunting Tests
Carting	Lure Coursing
Conformation	Obedience
Coonhound Events	Schutzhund
Earthdog	Tracking
Field Trials	Water Dog

Most breeders have a main area of interest. If you hope to do more with your dog than simply have a family pet, you should find breeders whose strengths fall in the area you are also interested in. If your interest is hunting, for example, then look for a breeder who is knowledgeable and produces successful hunting dogs.

Other people may enjoy working in several areas of competition. This does not mean that a dog from a breeder who specializes in one area cannot be trained in another sport, but you should look at the dog's background to see what type of competitions the parents have competed in. A background that shows titles in obedience, agility, and a working sport at least gives you an indication of the dog's potential trainability. And it shows you that this breeder's dogs have been successfully tested and measure up against other dogs.

What Was Your Goal in Breeding This Litter?

The responsible breeder's overall goal should be to improve the breed in temperament, structure, soundness, and working ability—not just "the dog has a great temperament" or "my Sparky is so sweet." She should have specific goals in mind. For instance, my goal is to have versatile dogs who can work in several areas of competition, while another breeder might be content to improve her dog's working abilities alone. Some breeders may be very specific about their goals: Perhaps they need to strengthen the rear structure of their breeding stock or bring more boldness or speed into their hunting dogs.

There is no right answer, as long as the breeder has a specific goal in mind with each breeding—one that aims to breed better dogs.

What Are the Registered Names of the Sire and Dam?

Titles become part of a dog's name and are listed on the pedigree. Conformation titles appear before the name, while performance titles appear after the name. Ch. Bubchen's Liebchen V. Kleefeld, NSD, NRD, SD, RD, SDX, CD, VX has titles earned through the AKC and through the Weimaraner Club of America (WCA). The AKC titles are Ch. (Championship, a conformation title) and CD (Companion Dog, in obedience). The WCA titles are all in hunting: NSD (Novice Shooting Dog), SD (Shooting Dog), NRD (Novice Retrieving Dog), RD (Retrieving Dog), SDX (Shooting Dog Excellent), and VX (Versatility Excellent). When looking at the titles, you can see that this dog competed in three areas of competition—conformation, obedience, and field. Such a dog in a puppy's pedigree suggests that at least some of these talents will be passed on.

When studying the breed of your choice, check the national club's Web site to get a list of the titles it offers. That knowledge can give you a better idea of the potential of the offspring and the direction the breeder is going in with her breeding program.

Do You Own Both Parents? Can I Meet Them?

It's always a good idea, if possible, to meet a pup's parents, because their temperament will tell you a lot about what kind of dog their puppy will grow up to be. The breeder should have the dam but not necessarily the sire at her kennel. (The sire is the father of the puppies and the dam is the mother.) Breeders will often use a male from another kennel to improve or complement their own lines. It's not unusual to find out that the sire lives in California, while you are looking at puppies in Pennsylvania. Ask

BSP Ch. Aranars Nordic Giddy Up 'N Go, a Weimaraner owned by the author.

why the breeder chose that particular stud dog. This will also give you an idea of the goals of her breeding program.

Is the sire the breeder's own dog? Occasionally, that makes for a good match, but I would be suspicious if the breeder only bred her own males to her own females, because the gene pool becomes too small and health and temperament problems can arise.

How Many Litters Have This Sire and Dam Produced Together?

This is an important question to help determine whether she is breeding so many dogs that she could be called a mini puppy mill. If this person is breeding the same dogs season after season, she is probably just in it for the money. Generally, breeding the same dogs every season does not move a breed forward or move a person's own breeding program to the next level.

It is not unusual for a reputable breeder to rebreed a particular combination of dogs if the resulting puppies were of excellent quality. But if it is a first-time breeding of the pair, breeders generally wait twelve months or more to evaluate how their offspring fared against other dogs in competition before trying the same breeding again. Breeding the same dogs each time the bitch comes in season, which is usually a six-month interval, is not enough time to determine whether the puppies will measure up. This is a major red flag.

How Old Are the Parents?

This is an important question, especially for breeds that require health certifications. Some breeds should be certified clear of hip dysplasia, for example, which can only be done after the dogs are two years old. Other breeds should be tested for eye problems, thyroid function, soundness in the elbows and knees, and so on. The Web site of the national breed club is a great source for this information. If the national club requires or strongly encourages the certification of dogs used in breeding programs, then make sure you are aware of the age requirements for certification, how often the tests must be done, and the results of the parents of the litter you are interested in and the littermates of the parents.

Are the Parents Cleared for Hip Dysplasia?

Clearance comes from either the Orthopedic Foundation for Animals (OFA) or the University of Pennsylvania Hip Improvement Program (PennHIP). If a breeder hasn't heard of either of these, beware. My favorite question to ask breeders is, "Is your dog OFA-certified for hips?" More often than not, the answer I receive is "Yes, they're AKC registered." This is a major red flag, because the AKC has nothing to do with OFA. If the breeder replies, "Yes, the parents are OFA certified," be sure to ask, "How old are they?" because they must be at least two years old. Also be sure to ask to see the clearance certificate of both dogs. Make sure the names on the certificates match the name of the parents of the puppies.

The most common registry is OFA, which maintains databases, sorted by breed, of dogs that have been tested for soundness in their hips, knees, and elbows, hearing, thyroid and heart function, and genetic markers for certain other inheritable conditions. Results of the various tests can be viewed on the OFA Web site so that you can research the sire and dam of the litter you are interested in before purchasing a puppy. You can also view the extended canine family members so that you can see how those animals tested.

To receive an OFA clearance, the owner must submit an X-ray of the hips when the dog is at least two years old. The X-ray is taken in a prescribed position, and then orthopedic specialists read it and compare their findings with other dogs of the same breed and age range. This test need only be done once during the dog's lifetime.

Training dogs to the highest performance levels can be very expensive, and breeders do not want to put money into training a dog who may not be physically sound enough for top competition. That's why some breeders will do a preliminary assessment of a young dog's hips before beginning rigorous training. However, a preliminary assessment *should not* replace the certificate issued by OFA.

There are three possible ratings for dogs with passing hips: excellent, which means the hip joint is especially sound; good, which means the hips are above average hips for that age and breed of dog (most dogs fall into this category); and fair, which means the hips are average when compared with dogs of the same breed and age range. Dogs with passing hips receive a registration number and a certificate showing the dog's name, birth date, sire, dam, date of X-ray, age of dog when tested, and the rating. These numbers are not easy to read if you don't know what you're looking at. For example, the number VZ-8447G29M-PI means:

VZ—Vizsla (this two-letter abbreviation will vary by breed)

8447—Certificate number

G—Good (the rating)

29—Age, in months, of the dog when certified

M—Male (the sex)

PI—The dog is permanently identified with a tattoo or microchip (NOPI means No Permanent Identification)

In addition, the certificate shows the microchip or tattoo number, application number, date of report, color of the dog, and his name.

Only dogs receiving an excellent, good, or fair rating should be used in breeding programs. To help a breed's hips become healthier overall, many breeders make it a policy not to breed a dog with fair hips and opt only for those with good or excellent hips. But sometimes a dog with many outstanding characteristics but only fair hips will be bred to a dog with excellent hips, in the hopes of producing puppies who carry the best traits of each parent. Remember, fair hips are not an indication of the disorder, but it is a way some breeders raise the bar for breeding excellence.

Dogs who do not pass the certification also receive grades for their hips. Dogs testing as borderline dysplastic are usually reevaluated several months later, because a borderline grade could be due to poor X-rays. A rating of mild dysplastic means the hips show minor changes and abnormalities, which may include arthritis. Dogs rated as moderate usually show signs of lameness and pain. Dogs rated as severe are candidates for hip replacement surgery. None of these dogs should be bred, no matter what other wonderful traits they possess. And Dr. Jason Randall of the Animal Hospital of Woodstock, Illinois, advises prospective puppy purchasers not to buy a puppy who comes from parents who have not had their hips certified.

The second registry breeders can use for hip certification is PennHIP. As with OFA, X-rays are used to evaluate hips, which are then given a numerical score. Some breeders feel the PennHIP evaluation method is more accurate in predicting the onset of osteoarthritis, which is a degenerative joint disease and a sign of hip dysplasia. PennHIP can be performed on dogs as young as 16 weeks, as the hip laxity at that age is comparable to the laxity when the dog reaches maturity. It is recommended that young dogs be tested several times to receive a more reliable reading.

Because hip dysplasia is caused by a complex interaction of several genes, plus some environmental factors, currently no breeder can completely eliminate it from every dog she breeds. Even dogs who pass certification tests may carry the gene and can pass the problem along. Still, responsible breeders X-ray their dogs and breed only those dogs who receive clearances. Overall, the incidence of hip dysplasia has declined in breeds whose breeders are active in the certification process. Although certifications are not foolproof, you know the breeder is doing all she can to improve her breeding program and the breed in general.

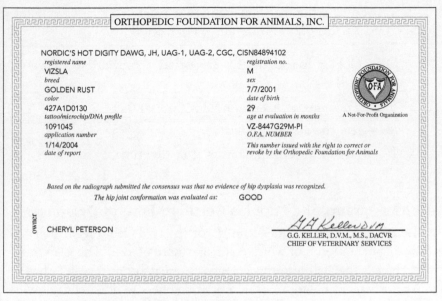

ORTHOPEDIC FOUNDATION FOR ANIMALS, INC.

NORDIC'S HOT DIGITY DAWG, JH, UAG-1, UAG-2, CGC, CISN84894102
registered name   *registration no.*
VIZSLA   M
breed   *sex*
GOLDEN RUST   7/7/2001
color   *date of birth*
427A1D0130   29
tattoo/microchip/DNA profile   *age at evaluation in months*   A Not-For-Profit Organization
1091045   VZ-8447G29M-PI
application number   *O.F.A. NUMBER*
1/14/2004   *This number issued with the right to correct or*
date of report   *revoke by the Orthopedic Foundation for Animals*

Based on the radiograph submitted the consensus was that no evidence of hip dysplasia was recognized.
The hip joint conformation was evaluated as: GOOD

owner

CHERYL PETERSON   G.G. KELLER, D.V.M., M.S., DACVR
                                             CHIEF OF VETERINARY SERVICES

Certificate from the Orthopedic Foundation for Animals.

Are the Parents Certified Clear of Eye Problems?

In breeds suffering from eye disorders, responsible breeders have the eyes of all their breeding stock certified by the Canine Eye Registration Foundation (CERF). This organization maintains a database of all certified dogs, and the results of all dogs tested through the program are used in research so that eye diseases can be monitored by breed. Dogs who are not cleared should not be bred.

Dogs must be examined by board-certified ophthalmologists to be certified as clear, and the examination must be repeated every year. If the breed you are interested in has a high incidence of eye problems (see chapter 4), ask to see a copy of the clearances on both parents and examine the certificate to make sure the names on the certificates match the names of the parents. Make sure the certificate is not more than one year old, as well.

Dogs who pass the CERF examination receive a clearance number such as GR1857/89-102. This would be read as follows:

GR—Golden Retriever (this two-letter abbreviation will vary by breed)

857—The number dog of that breed tested that year

/89—Year the dog was tested

102—Age of the dog in months at testing time

Are the Parents and Puppies Certified Free of Deafness?

Although congenital deafness can occur in any breed, breeds that have white pigmentation and white coats are more at risk. There are eighty AKC breeds that fall into this category. Research has revealed that two genes are responsible for most inherited deafness in dogs, both of which are linked to coat color. The first is the merle gene, which is found in Collies, Shetland Sheepdogs, Australian Cattle Dogs, Australian Shepherds, Cardigan Welsh Corgis, Great Danes with the harlequin pattern, Dachshunds with the dapple pattern, and other breeds. (The merle coat pattern has irregular dark blotches against a lighter background of the same basic color.) The second is the piebald gene, found in such breeds as the Bull Terrier, Great Pyrenees, Akita, Beagle, and Dalmatian. (Piebald coats have irregular black patches on a white background.)

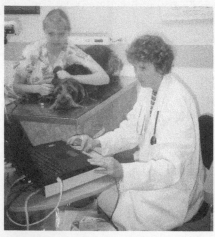

Joann Randall, D.V.M., performing a BAER test.

Not every dog with these coat patterns is deaf, but deafness is more common in dogs with these coats—which is why the breeder should make sure the parents and the puppies are all tested. If the puppies have a deaf parent, a test is also important. Puppies can be evaluated for hearing loss at 35 days of age. If the litter was tested, the breeder should be able to show you the results.

The only accepted method of diagnosing deafness is the Brainstem Auditory Evoked Response (BAER) test, which detects electrical activity in the cochlea of the ear and auditory pathways in the brain. The test is performed by a board-certified veterinary neurologist or experienced veterinary audiologist. A printed result of the BAER test is given to the owner. This test only needs to be performed once during the dog's lifetime. Most national breed clubs maintain their own databases of which dogs pass or fail the test.

What Other Health Problems Have the Parents Been Tested For?

Certain breeds have specific medical problems that occur more often in their gene pool (see chapter 4), and some of them can be detected by genetic tests. Not every inherited disorder has a genetic test, but good breeders do all the testing they can. The national breed club usually lists these certifications on their Web site. Take the list with you when you visit a breeder, and ask about every test on it. Weeding out the irresponsible breeders is easier than having to deal with serious health problems down the road.

Can You Recommend a Veterinarian in My Area?

Just like physicians, not all veterinarians are created equal. When your dog needs medical attention, the last thing you want to worry about is how comfortable you are with the veterinarian's knowledge and experience with the breed and the problems associated with it. I suggest people use a veterinarian who is experienced with the breed of dog they own, since each breed has its own quirks. Some breeds are very sensitive to the use of anesthesia, for example, while others are sensitive to vaccinations. Veterinarians who know about your breed will usually recognize and treat symptoms faster than those who don't. Good breeders develop a very close relationship with their veterinarian, and the absence of such a relationship is a red flag.

If you cannot use the same veterinarian as your dog's breeder, ask her if she can recommend one near you. The chances are that if she does not know one personally, another breeder she knows may have a recommendation.

What Is the Price of a Puppy?

The price of a puppy is determined by how much demand there is for the breed, the pup's background, the reputation of the breeder, and the quality of the pup. When you find out how much the breeder is asking, be sure to also ask what factors affect that price.

High demand drives up the cost of a puppy, but the higher price does not always mean higher quality. Fad breeds that have recently been seen in movies and TV commercials may cost more simply because there may be many people asking for them. Remember the movie *101 Dalmatians*? So many people tried to cash in on the fad that the indiscriminate breeding programs inflicted many health problems that responsible breeders are still trying to correct. It can take a decade for dedicated breeders of an exploited breed to correct problems that have emerged due to irresponsible breeding.

A very rare breed may also cost more, simply because there are few of the dogs around. If only a handful of litters are bred each year, the people who want these puppies may be willing to pay a premium for them.

The quality of the dogs in the pedigree is another important factor in a puppy's price, and this is something that really matters. Does the pup have dual champions in his background? What about Registry of Merit (an award from a national breed club for dogs who consistently produce excellent offspring) dogs? Pedigrees containing animals of such distinction have usually been planned generation after generation by serious breeders. These decades of careful planning add to the price (and real value) of a puppy.

Each individual pup's potential to excel in the show ring, in canine sports, or in both, also affects the price. Breeders will carefully evaluate a litter and decide which are the show- or competition-quality puppies and which are the pet-quality puppies. Pet quality simply means the traits the dog possesses are not at competition level. The flaw could be something very superficial, such as a splash of white on the chest or a little kink in the tail. Unless you plan to compete with your dog, this is no big deal. Pet-quality puppies from a responsible breeder are still temperamentally and physically sound and will make a great addition to your family. Most breeders reduce their price a bit for a pet-quality puppy. Many breeders also require that he be spayed or neutered and/or sold on limited registration (see page 108). Still, it costs as much to feed, vaccinate, and care for a pet pup as it does to raise his show-quality littermates, so don't expect a huge price reduction.

Don't be fooled by unscrupulous breeders or pet shops who tell you that a pup's price is high because he is a "rare" color or color combination, or because he has "special" markings or an "unusual" coat. Beware of particolored Poodles, white Boxers, Labrador Retrievers with white spots, blue Weimaraners, and other so-called "rare" specimens. This is one way bad breeders get rid of dogs who do not conform to the breed standard. This is why it is so important to read the breed standard (see chapter 4); if you feel the need, bring the standard along with you when you go to meet breeders.

Where Are the Registration Papers?

While I have already explained in chapter 5 why registration with any kennel club is no guarantee of quality, you are still entitled to see proof that the dogs you are looking at are the breed they are represented as

Whippet puppies play with Daniel and Terrence.

being. The only way to do that is with registration papers. When a litter is bred, the breeder sends in a form in to the AKC (or another registry) recording the birth of the litter and detailing the names and registration numbers of the parents, how many puppies were born, their color, and their sex. The breeder gets back an individual registration slip for each puppy. She should give this slip to you when you buy the pup, and you must fill it in and send it back, along with a fee, to register your new dog. (If the breeder had already registered all the pups, which is not common, she must send in a change of ownership form when you buy a puppy.)

If a breeder tells you she doesn't have the papers yet, *do not buy the dog.* Never accept a promise that the papers will be along later. A breeder who is conscientious about her paperwork will have all the puppy registration slips on hand by the time she is ready to sell her dogs. If the papers never turn up, the AKC cannot intervene, and you may have little recourse through the courts. If you buy a purebred puppy, get the papers with the pup.

Be aware that there is more than one type of AKC registration. The most common is full registration. This form of registration transfers all rights, including the breeding of the dog, directly to you.

Another form is limited registration. A dog sold on a limited registration cannot be shown in conformation, but he can compete in other AKC sports. His offspring cannot be registered either; this is intended as a deterrent to breeding. The AKC instituted this form of registration in

AKC registration for Ch. Aranars Nordic Giddy Up 'N Go.

1989 to help breeders protect their dogs against irresponsible breeding. If the dog proves to be a beautiful specimen, the breeder can change the designation to full registration, thus allowing the dog all the privileges of that status.

Limited registration is not a punishment or an indication that a dog is bad. The AKC encourages breeders to discuss this option fully with puppy buyers, so that there are no misunderstandings. Make sure you understand your dog's registration, because *the AKC will not get involved in disagreements between breeders and owners*.

If you get your dog from a rescue organization or a shelter, registration may not be possible because the group may not know who the dog's parents are. Indefinite Listing Privileges, more commonly known as an ILP number, will enable you to compete in canine sports (again, except conformation) with your dog, although he must be neutered. The application for an ILP number is available on the AKC Web site. You must send it in along with two color photographs, proof that the dog has been altered, and the application fee. Only dogs of a fully recognized breed can be registered. ILP numbers are also available for dogs registered with the AKC's Foundation Stock Service (see appendix A).

What Are the Terms of Your Contract?

More and more breeders are using a contract that spells out exactly what their responsibilities are and what yours are. A contract is a good thing, because with it everyone knows exactly where they stand on a variety of issues, including what happens if a puppy turns out to have a genetic disorder, breeding rights, the breeder's return policy, and so forth. Some states now require puppy sales contracts.

Read the contract all the way through before you sign it and make sure you understand every provision. If you don't understand something, ask. An honest, responsible breeder should be happy to explain her contract to you.

What If the Puppy Has a Medical Problem?

Most contracts require you to visit a veterinarian within a specified period of time to have the puppy checked for obvious health problems. If any are found, your remedy from the breeder may be the return of the puppy,

Co-Ownership

Sometimes dogs are co-owned, which means two or more people share all the rights of ownership. The signature of all owners is needed to register the dog with the AKC, to transfer ownership, or to register a litter. Co-ownership can work very well when the career of the dog requires a fairly large investment, or when a more experienced dog fancier is guiding the career of a novice. Many times a group of people will co-own a particular dog and share the expenses, and the glory, if the dog proves to be one of the elite in the dog world.

The AKC discourages co-ownership, however, because when the co-owners disagree about competition ideals, breeding decisions, or division of expenses, things can get contentious. The AKC has no power to get involved in or resolve these kinds of disagreements, and breeding or sporting careers can be halted indefinitely while the various parties fight things out in court. On the legal side, if the dog bites someone all the co-owners can be sued, even if the dog was not under their control or living with them.

If you are buying a puppy you intend to show extensively or compete with seriously, and if that puppy will ultimately be part of a careful, well-thought-out breeding program, it's not unreasonable for the breeder to be a co-owner so she can have a say in the dog's career. If, however, you are buying a puppy to be your family pet, there is no reason for the breeder to co-own the dog.

a cash allowance, replacement of the puppy, or payment of medical expenses to correct a condition such as a hernia. These terms should be spelled out clearly in the contract.

If you wait past that time to take the puppy in for his checkup, the breeder can claim any subsequent illnesses developed after you took your dog home. And if you allow the puppy to get into your child's toys or something toxic and the dog becomes ill, you cannot expect the breeder to assume any responsibility. However, if the puppy becomes ill some time after his initial exam due to a genetic or hereditary problem, you should have some recourse with the breeder—which the contract should spell out.

What If I Cannot Keep the Dog?

Reputable breeders will take a dog back and find an appropriate home for him—*for the life of the dog*. They do this because they care deeply about the fate of every dog they breed. The AKC also requires breeders to keep accurate records of their puppy sales, and most breeders want to know where their puppies are. Depending on the age of the dog, you may receive a portion of your money back, but there is no standard practice among breeders. This is a topic that should be covered in the contract, to avoid any questions down the road.

Is There a Spay/Neuter Clause?

It is not unusual for a puppy to be sold on a spay/neuter contract, especially if the puppy has traits (superficial or otherwise) that should not be passed on. The conditions of such a clause will vary from breeder to breeder. Many times, a spay/neuter clause is used in conjunction with limited

registration. So, for example, when a dog reaches a certain age and the breeder decides he would not be competitive in the show ring, the contract requires that the owner spay or neuter the dog.

Breeders should fully explain this clause in the contract and the reasoning behind it to you. Many reputable breeders want to curb the use of dogs in indiscriminate breeding programs. It is hard to blame a breeder for taking such measures, since her reputation can be haunted by puppy owners who breed their dogs with little or no thought or care.

Nothing's more fun than a lapful of puppies!

What If I Want to Breed My Dog?

Consider carefully whether your dog is actually breeding material. Your dog should be able to prove himself to a high standard in whatever activity his breed was developed to do. If you have a hunting breed, for example, you should be able to get a Senior Hunter title on your dog (not just a Junior Hunter, which is very basic work). This higher level shows that the dog is trainable, has the right instincts, and may pass on those traits. He should also excel in the show ring, where his basic soundness will be judged.

Breeders should encourage their puppy owners to prove the quality of their dog through competition and mentor them through the process. If your dog proves himself, the breeder can also help you decide if he should be bred and help select prospective breeding partners that will complement your dog. Your dog's breeder knows the various lines in the breed and what they produce, and whether a particular dog would be a good match for your dog.

However, just because the puppy has great drive in field work or does well in obedience does not mean he should be bred—or that you should be a breeder. Ask yourself: Why would anyone want to buy a dog from me?

Jeremy Brick and his dog Jig go through the paces together on an agility course.

If you cannot place all the puppies in homes, are you prepared to keep the remaining puppies? Or will you be irresponsible and take them to the local shelter for its personnel to deal with? Ask yourself, "Am I the kind of responsible breeder described in this book?"

Some Thoughts about Spaying and Neutering

If you do not want to compete in conformation with your dog, or if your dog does not measure up to the breed standard, there's no reason not to spay or neuter the dog. It is the best way to ensure the dog's health and your peace of mind. The benefits of spaying or neutering your dog are great.

- You avoid the messy cycle a female goes through (during the female's heat cycle, she discharges blood and scent).

- The male's desire to wander is curbed (the scent of a female in heat can bring an intact male to her doorstep from several miles away).

- It greatly reduces the risk of mammary cancer and eliminates the risk of pyometra (an often fatal infection of the uterus) and uterine cancer in females.

- It greatly reduces the risk of prostate cancer and eliminates the risk of testicular cancer in males.

- It reduces interdog aggression.

- It reduces dominance aggression toward people.

- It helps reduce marking and mounting behavior in males.

- It prevents unwanted pregnancies.

With all the unwanted and abandoned puppies and dogs that are put to death throughout the country each year, do you really want to add to that problem?

Perhaps you're thinking, "I spent $500 on the dog. Maybe I can get that back, or even more, if I breed a litter or two." Think again. Breeding a litter and doing it the right way—as a responsible breeder—will cost you a considerable amount of money, as the table on page 114 illustrates.

What Does It Cost to Breed a Litter?	
Health exam before breeding	$75
OFA certification	$100
CERF certification	$75
Ovulation testing	$150
Stud fee	$500 (or more!)
Prenatal exams (including ultrasound)	$300
Puppy exams and shots	$300
Miscellaneous items	$200
Total	$1,700*

* Does not include any complications during pregnancy or delivery, or the cost of all the furniture and carpeting in your house that a litter of puppies can destroy.

Problems can develop during pregnancy that will require more ultrasounds and other diagnostic measures, and possibly a cesarean delivery. Add this cost to the cost of a puppy requiring additional medical attention, worming the litter, postdelivery examination of the female, and any other problems the female or puppies may encounter, such as infections or a virus—it's not cheap! Plus, do not forget the amount of time and energy you will expend to take care of the litter, including feeding, cleaning, socializing, and placing the puppies.

Then ask yourself: Why would someone want to buy a dog from me when they can get a quality animal of proven stock from an experienced breeder? Spay or neuter your pet and leave the art of breeding to those who are knowledgeable.

7

Bringing Your Dog Home

You've chosen a breed you feel is right for your family, you've chosen a breeder you feel comfortable with, and now you've chosen a puppy as well. But bringing your puppy home is not as simple as just bundling him into the car and then carrying him into the house. There's a lot you must do before you bring your new dog home, and even more work to help your dog adjust to your family.

A Pet-Safe House

Before bringing your dog home, you must make sure your house is pet safe. If your children have oodles of plastic toys, perhaps a new house rule is that those toys stay in the kids' bedrooms and the doors must be closed. This way your dog cannot grab and start chewing something that could pose a danger to him.

To keep him from drinking out of the toilet bowl, make sure everyone in the household knows to put the lid down or close the door behind them when leaving the bathroom. Make sure pantyhose and similar items are kept away from the dog as well. These items can really cause serious problems if swallowed.

Also check to see where the garbage is located, especially kitchen garbage, which contains food scraps your dog will not be able to resist. The location may be convenient for you, but it may also be convenient for the dog to get into and drag all over the house, eating items he should not have along the way.

What about cabinet doors? Can they be opened by a curious dog? Maybe childproof latches are the answer—especially in the kitchen and bathrooms, where toxic items are stored.

Puppies chew on everything, including electrical cords, boxes of tissues, books, and the TV remote. Until your dog passes though his chewing phase, cover or put away all these items.

Where do you plan to put the dog's crate? Check to make sure he cannot reach electrical cords or outlets with his tongue. You will be amazed how long those tongues can be!

Dog-proofing a house is similar to childproofing. Get down to the pup's level and look around. If something looks like it could be dangerous, then it probably is. Take precautions before your dog comes home.

Essential Supplies

You'll need to go shopping *before* you bring your dog home. The essential supplies I list here should already be on hand when he arrives.

- *Food and water dishes.* Dishes for food and water come in all types and sizes. I prefer stainless steel bowls over weighted dishes and those that come in racks, because the stainless steel dishes are easy to clean and almost impossible to break.

- *Leash.* A six-foot leather leash will be very helpful when walking the dog and training him. I prefer leather over nylon, because a nylon leash can hurt your hands if the dog pulls.

- *Collars.* You'll need two types of collars. One is a buckle collar with identification tags attached, which should be worn at all times. This collar will not choke the dog if it becomes tangled in something. The second is a choke collar, also sometimes called a training collar because it is easy with this type of collar to quickly correct the dog. This should only be used when you are training and walking the dog. Your dog should never wear his choke collar when he is left unattended, including in his crate, in the car, or alone in the yard, because if the collar or leash gets caught on something, he could panic and choke himself to death trying to get free. So do be careful. When choosing a choke collar, make sure the links in the collar are smooth. Once the collar is on, you should have approximately two extra inches of link length. You should be able to pull on the collar and release it with a very smooth working action. Cheap collars do not release as easily, and when you pull on them, you can hear the links clink.

- *Crate*. This is an indispensable training tool, and will also become your dog's safe haven. Choose a sturdy crate that is easy to clean and large enough for your puppy to stand up, turn around, and lie down in. See the section on crate training later in this chapter for more advice on buying a crate.

- *Grooming tools*. You need a good, sharp set of nail cutters. There are a variety of nail cutters on the market; ask your dog's breeder or a professional groomer for a recommendation. Whatever style you choose should be appropriate for the size of the nail you are cutting. If the cutters are too small, they will get caught or bend the nail, causing pain to your pet. You should also have a bottle of Kwik Stop to stop bleeding nails if you accidentally cut too deep. Other items to have on hand are a brush, and possibly a comb if he's a long-haired dog. Brushing at least once each week will keep your dog's coat neat and clean. Brushing removes dead hair, distributes natural skin oils, and stimulates blood circulation—the same good things brushing your hair does for you. The comb is used to take out mats and tangles. The dog may need to be clipped or trimmed periodically, and if so you will need special grooming tools for this. Your research into breeds should tell you more precisely what kind of grooming tools your dog requires, and your dog's breeder should be very helpful in this area.

- *Chews*. Dogs must chew, especially puppies. When choosing chews for your dog, make sure you get something that won't break or crumble off in little bits, which the dog can swallow and choke on. Very hard plastic bones are a good choice, as are large beef bones (the kind you'd get from the butcher, not small steak bones). A good, hard bone is also best to help keep your dog's teeth clean. Once the flavor has worn off, you can make them more enticing by stuffing the middle with peanut butter or cheese. Dogs love rawhide bones, too, but take care not to let your dog eat the bone all in one sitting. Rawhide can cause problems in the digestive tract if the dog eats too much. And pieces of the rawhide can become caught in your dog's throat, so once it's down to the knot, get rid of it. It is usually best to let the dog have a rawhide for about twenty minutes at a time (supervised by you), and then replace it with a hard bone.

- *Toys.* Puppies love toys, but watch for unsafe items such as plastic eyes that can be swallowed and cause blockages. Many toys come with squeakers, which dogs can tear out and swallow. When buying toys, use common sense, as you would with young children, and supervise playtime to make it safe. Dogs will eventually destroy their toys, and that's something you need to just resign yourself to. As each toy is torn apart, replace it with a new one.

- *Dog food.* The next section will help you choose among the many dog foods available.

This Canaan Dog puppy has toys, a dish, and a new friend on his first day home.

Feeding Your Dog

Buying a good dog food is a major investment in your dog's ongoing health. Quality food is expensive—$1 or $2 a pound—but cheap food is also cheap from a nutritional standpoint. And it may even be more expensive in the long run, because you have to feed your dog larger portions of a cheap food to give him all the nutrients he needs. Better foods with better-quality ingredients require much smaller portions. The proof is in the poop: Your dog's stools should be well formed and darkish in color, which indicates that his body is processing all the nutrients in the food. If your dog's stools are not well formed or are light in color, the dog is not properly processing the food. This is often the case with inexpensive brands. So it actually costs less in the long run to feed your dog a better-quality food because you feed him less and, since he is digesting the food properly, there is less, shall we say, yard maintenance.

Generally, the cheaper brands contain sugar to entice the dog to eat. From time to time, I receive calls from people who say their dog is hyperactive. Quite often, the problem is a combination of not enough exercise and too much sugar. If you have children, you know that when you feed your child Froot Loops, his energy level goes up. And hyperactive kids are advised to avoid sugar altogether.

Switching to a high-quality food—the expensive brands that are not available at the grocery store—will make a big difference in your dog's health and behavior. Ask your dog's breeder and your veterinarian for recommendations.

Permanent Identification

One of the worst things that can happen to a family is losing their pet. You know the scenario: posters go up, the police and shelters are contacted, and the kids run up and down the block yelling the dog's name while dad jumps in the car to search and mom stays near the telephone. If someone finds the dog, or if he turns up at a shelter, a tag on his collar with your name and phone number will help him get home. But tags can fall off or, through wear and weather, become illegible. That's why it's also a good idea to consider microchipping, a form of permanent identification.

A microchip is a tiny transponder, about the size of a grain of rice, encased in sterile glass. It is placed under the skin between your dog's shoulder blades by the veterinarian, and remains there for the life of your dog. Each chip has a unique number. When a microchip reader is passed over the transponder, it reads and displays the chip's number.

That information is useless by itself, though, which is why you must register the number with a microchip recovery service. The best-known program is the AKC Companion Animal Recovery (CAR) program, known as Home Again. When you register, the number is stored in a database with the your contact information and other pertinent information about the dog. The information will also include your veterinarian's name and phone number, along with a contact you designate if you are unreachable. The Home Again program tracks tattoo numbers as well as microchips. All companion animals can be registered, including cats, birds, horses, and exotic animals.

Crate Training

Make sure you have a crate ready *before* you bring your puppy home. You have undoubtedly heard stories about dogs destroying everything from shoes to furniture when they were left unattended. Destruction is, unfortunately, one of the main reasons dogs lose their homes. Dogs left uncrated tend to become bored of chewing their bone and search for items with your scent on it, such as your shoes, to chew on. They can ingest things that are not really digestible and become sick. Then you come home to little surprises all over the house.

Crates also provide safety for your dog when traveling. Whenever your dog rides in a car, he should be in a crate. This protects the dog from being tossed around the car if you make a sudden stop or are involved in an accident. It also keeps him contained so you don't have to worry about him wanting to sit in your lap or barking at fellow travelers. In addition, when vacationing, many motels will only allow a dog in the room if he is crated.

Sometimes people who decide to use a crate to help train their dog feel horrible about leaving him in such a small space. This guilt often leads them to buy a crate that is much too large, which defeats the purpose. Crating a dog is not cruel. In the wild dogs sleep in dens about the size of a crate. A crate is just a substitute for your dog's den, except it's in your house with the luxuries of air conditioning and heat to make him comfortable. Crates also provide a sense of security and a place the dog can go to get away from the kids if he's tired or not feeling well. Children should be instructed never to play inside the dog's crate or bother the dog while he's in his "bedroom."

Dogs instinctively keep their dens clean—which is why a crate is such an excellent house training tool. However, if you put a small puppy in a large crate, he has room to mess at one end and lie down at other end, far from his mess. Thus, a large crate may confuse your dog into thinking this is the "indoor facilities." (This is why it is important to make sure you take the puppy out regularly, before he has time to mess in his crate. So when he wakes up from his nap, he needs to go outside pronto!)

A crate should be large enough for him to stand up and turn around in, and to be able to lie down with his legs outstretched, but no larger. A good general rule is to buy a crate that is two to four inches taller than the height of your dog at his shoulders—when he is an adult. That means you will need to know how tall he is going to be when he reaches his adult height. Your dog's breeder should be able to help you with this information. Washable bedding is a good idea for inside the crate.

Crates can be made of molded plastic (required for shipping dogs by air) or heavy metal wire. Either kind is good for housebreaking. Crates must be chosen carefully, as there are many styles that can be unsafe for your pet. One unsafe style has large pins at each corner holding the side, front, and back panels together through eyelets. These pins tend to loosen and pop out of the eyelets. This gives the dog a spot that he may be able to push hard enough for his head to go

Claire helps Millie get used to her new home.

through and get caught. Another unsafe style has a top that latches by pushing the side of the crate in and positioning hook-type endings on the top portion. Once you release the pressure, the latches are supposed to interlock as the crate closes. Some dogs can push these crates open at the top and get their heads stuck.

For a wire crate, I suggest a suitcase style, because you don't have to worry about pins or top-latching devices. The whole crate is already put together. All you have to do is unfold the crate and it's ready to use. These crates can be found through specialty catalogs and online.

Plastic crates have air holes for air circulation but are more enclosed. This can help a dog feel safer and will also keep him warmer in the winter, but he can more easily overheat in the summer. The metal wire crates provide good air circulation and can be covered to keep out drafts, if necessary. Some dogs seem to like being able to see out of the metal crates, while others like being hidden in the plastic crates.

To introduce your puppy to his new crate, drop treats in the back of the crate every few hours, and let him explore it by himself.

You can teach your dog to enjoy his crate. As in house training, you simply need to set up a routine. The first part of the routine is training him to accept his crate and making his time in it a good experience. Feed him in the crate and toss treats into it to make it easier for him to accept. Talk to him gently when he is quiet inside, telling him what a good boy he is. Give him a chew toy, so he can keep himself occupied in the crate.

With my dogs, their routine starts off each morning going directly out to potty and play. Then they eat their morning meal. Once they have eaten, I toss treats in the crate and praise them as they go in. Since the breeds I have can suffer from bloat (see chapter 4), which is a twisting of the stomach, the house rule is after they have eaten they sleep for an hour. They know the routine, so when they finish their meal, they run and sit in front of their crates waiting for that treat. Their built-in alarm clock actually wakes them up approximately an hour later and they go out again. (A puppy will need a quick potty break right after eating—see the house training section that follows. An adult, however, can easily wait an hour.)

If your dog whines in the crate, try turning a radio on in the room with soothing music or voices.

By the time the puppy is twelve weeks old, he should be able to make it through an eight-hour night of sleep in his crate. If he wakes up and you hear him fussing in the crate, he may be telling you he has to go out. After you put him out and he finishes his business, put him right back to bed to finish his nap, and do not forget to praise him for asking to go out.

House Training

House training really is not difficult, but it is time-consuming and requires discipline and commitment to a routine from all family members. It's best to make a house training plan before your dog comes home, assigning specific scheduled outings to individual family members, so everyone understands their responsibilities.

The whole process, as in all dog training, rests upon a routine. Your puppy must be taken out immediately when he wakes up in the morning and after naps, five minutes after he eats, and immediately after he plays. Remember that his bladder and bowels are small, so he needs to go more frequently than an adult dog. Set up a daily routine for taking him out to avoid accidents, and you'll find housetraining will be a breeze!

Take him out as you say the word "out" or "potty," so he starts to equate the word with the action. These outside potty trips should be all business— no playtime or cuddling. After he has finished his business, praise him. Then, if you want, you can have a few minutes of play. If you want to train him to eliminate in a specific area, take him to that area each and every time. If the spot is on your property, leave a tiny bit of stool behind (pick up most of it) so he'll have a visual and scent reminder for next time. After some repetition, he will get the idea and go to that area.

People used to paper-train their dog as part of the process of house training. And these days, puppy "wee wee pads" are sold in stores to aid in the process. But I do not recommend paper training. You already have a puppy piddling in the house; do you really want to use these pads to teach him to potty someplace else in the house? It is better to teach him to go outside right from the start.

While it is a good idea to clean up after your dog no matter where he goes (it's just cleaner and healthier), when you take your dog for walks off your property you absolutely *must* pick up after him. Sandwich bags work best for this. By placing one hand into the bag, you can pick up the feces and, using your other hand, gently pull the bag over your hand. This enables you to turn the bag inside out without coming in contact with the contents. Then all you have to do is dispose of the bag in the trash. If you live in an apartment, make sure your dog never urinates on any plantings or in the garden of your building by taking him directly to the street when you first get outside. Feeding the puppy stimulates his digestive tract, so approximately five minutes after he has finished his food, take him out to the designated area using the word you chose for this activity. Again, once he's completed his task, praise, praise, praise.

The stimulation of play gets the process going again. Usually, a pup will play and then sniff a couple of times, then play and then, oops! About ten minutes into an indoor play period, you need to tell the dog your chosen word and take him out. Again, praise him over and over when he does the right thing. Make a big deal out of it.

Growing puppies are a lot like growing children, and they need plenty of rest to make up for the energy they expend. After his play period, your pup will probably want to take a nap. After he wakes up, it's out again, using your chosen word. Praise him again for a job well done.

Getting him to go out *before* he has an accident in the house reinforces the idea that when he feels the urge, that's when he goes out. It's all a matter of timing. As he grows, he will be able to wait longer and longer, but still you need to keep up a routine.

It is not a good idea to leave water out for your puppy overnight. This just encourages him to drink and fill his bladder, after which you may have a mess to clean up. As long as he has received plenty of water throughout the day, he should be able to make it through the night without more. As the puppy grows, so will his control and the length of time he can hold his bladder.

One of the biggest mistakes people make is not properly reading the body language of their dog. Some dogs may sit by the door, while others stand in front of you staring, while others may bark or pace in circles. Each of these actions means he needs something, but it may not necessarily be a walk. Try using the special word that means it's time to go out to potty. If that is what he wants, he will perk up his ears and run to the door. You have trained him successfully!

I have received many calls from people whose dogs go upstairs into a bedroom to eliminate. Many times, the dog is trying to cover up the scent from a previous dog, either yours or that of the people who lived there before. This is easy to solve: Just close the doors to the rooms the dog should not be in.

Preparing for Visits to the Groomer and the Veterinarian

Preparing your dog for visits to the groomer and the veterinarian will make it less stressful on both your dog and the person working with him. When he is very young, you can help him get used to being handled by touching his feet, nails, and body.

Start with the toes and feet. When your puppy is having some quiet time, pick up a foot and rub it. When he allows this without a struggle, start to rub between his toes and hold and lightly squeeze his paw. Praise your puppy and reward him with treats. Repeat with each foot, stopping as soon as he begins to struggle. Eventually, you should be able to hold all four feet in turn.

Now it's time to keep the nail clippers handy. Take the clippers and touch his nails, rewarding and praising. Do not clip. Nails are very sensitive and, badly done, you'll hurt your dog and put him off the experience entirely.

The next part of the desensitizing process is introducing the puppy to various noises— of the kind small appliances at the grooming shop make. Start with the noise at a distance and slowly move it in closer, so that finally he sees the item making the noise. A good choice is a small, battery-operated tool, such as a power grinder. Start with the low speed. Let him see the tool, reinforcing good behavior with treats and praise.

Your next exercise is to start working to desensitize your puppy to body touching. With your dog standing, run your hand from his shoulder all the way down his back to his tail. Tell him to stand and stay and then praise him and give him a treat. Once he is over the wiggly stage and will stand and stay, add the front and rear legs, reminding him to stand and stay. After a few days, you should be able to touch the puppy over his entire body. Remember to praise and reward him along the way.

This Beagle has a bed full of toys and a crate.

Now for the next step. If you have an old electric razor, remove the blade so that only the buzzing of the razor is left. With the razor in your hand, use your hand as pressure, rubbing it down his back and legs. Remember, reward with praise and treats.

The next part of the desensitizing process is to place him on a small tabletop to help accustom him to being on the table at your veterinarian's office or at the groomer's. The dog needs to learn how to be quiet on the table, so that he does not fight, jump, or fall off, injuring himself. Before doing so, make sure you have a nonskid mat on the table for his safety. Start with the "stand" and "stay" commands, praising as you go. As he acclimates to the tabletop, praise him and then start again with the touchy-feely exercise over his body. Remember to touch his feet, toes, back, and legs. Then, when you feel he is comfortable with this exercise, add in the electric razor and a noise. If he struggles, go back a step and slowly reintroduce the progression of exercises again.

Nail Trimming

Keeping your dog's nails neatly trimmed will prevent accidental scratching of you and your belongings. And letting a dog's nails grow too long pushes back the natural stance of the foot, causing pain, lameness, and injury. But before you try to trim your dog's nails yourself, ask his breeder, groomer, or veterinarian to show you how.

Nail trimming should not hurt your dog, as long as you do not cut the quick. The quick is visible in white nails as a pink line running about three-quarters of the length of the nail, down the center. It carries the blood supply to the nail and will bleed profusely if you cut too much. In addition, the quick contains nerve endings and is extremely sensitive. So when you cut the nails, always cut *beyond* the quick.

If you did the desensitizing exercises, you should be able to hold your dog's foot gently in your hand. Start with just a small snip and remember to give him a treat. The dead nail will be brittle. Take another little snip and again reward him. You will know you are getting into healthy nail as the texture of the nail goes from brittle to a softer consistency.

Never make large cuts. If you look at the area you just cut, you will notice a small dot surfacing. That's the quick, which you want to avoid. If you accidentally cut too far and the nail begins to bleed, apply Kwik Stop, which is a form of styptic powder, to the end of the nail, and end the trimming session immediately with lots of hugs and treats. (In a pinch, cornstarch or drawing the nail across a bar of soap will also stop bleeding.)

Grooming Your Dog

Every dog needs to be brushed at least once a week, and dogs with longer coats will need daily brushing. Even if you regularly take your dog to a professional groomer, you need to do some upkeep to keep his coat in good shape. If you have a shorthaired dog, thorough brushing with a bristle brush once a week will be fine. When the dog is shedding more heavily in the spring and fall, daily brushing will help pull the dead coat out, leaving the new coat shining and less hair all over your home.

For longhaired breeds, you may need a variety of brushes and combs. Be sure to ask your dog's breeder what tools you'll need, and make sure she shows you how to use them. You will need to brush a longhaired dog at least three or four times a week. Brush the hair in layers, working in small sections from the foot to the top of the back. Do all four legs and then work your way up the shoulder. On the main body, again brush in sections, starting from the lowest point of the dog and moving upward to the top of the back.

For double-coated breeds, brush the hair thoroughly in sections at least twice a week. Make sure burrs and other foreign material are removed from the coat. It is important for you to separate the layers of coat and work down to the skin. If

This Belgian Shepherd puppy would like a bath, but it's not his turn!

you neglect the undercoat by not brushing down to the skin, the hair will matt, which is painful for the dog and difficult to comb out.

Wiry coats need to be brushed at least twice a week to remove dead hair. A bristle brush works best to accomplish this chore. Care must be taken not to break the hair; always brush it in the direction in which it grows.

For curly or wavy coats, use a fine wire slicker brush at least once a week. Start on the back legs and work forward by sections, separating the part that is done from what still needs to be brushed.

Don't forget to ask your dog's breeder or groomer for more advice on coat care, especially if you work your dog outdoors.

What You Need to Know About Your Dog's Health

No matter how wonderful your dog's veterinarian is, you must be involved with the healthcare of your pet. As the dog's owner, you will know if he is feeling great or if he is under the weather. Dogs can catch viruses that turn your bouncing puppy into a pooped pooch. They can ingest items that are not part of a canine diet, upsetting their stomachs or causing more serious problems. You are in the best position to notice changes in appetite and behavior that signal trouble.

You should learn to take your dog's temperature with a rectal thermometer. It is not much different than taking a baby's temperature. Coat the thermometer with a little baby oil and insert into the dog's rectum about an inch (less for little guys) for sixty seconds. You may have to gently hold the dog under the tummy while taking his temperature to keep him standing. A dog's normal temperature is between 100 degrees and 102.5 degrees Fahrenheit.

It is important to take your dog's temperature while he is healthy and at home, so you get an accurate reading and know exactly what his normal temperature is. For instance, I know my dogs' normal temperature is 101.3 degrees. When I see one of the dogs is not feeling well, the first thing I do is take his temperature. If the dog is running a fever, I know something is wrong. If the dog is listless, this is another sign that he is ill. If the dog is not feeling better in a few hours, it's time to call the vet.

Sore Muscle or Serious Illness?

One winter morning I took a dog out running in the field, and that evening he began to act strangely. He hunched his back and he was running a fever of 103.5 degrees. At first, I wasn't sure if the dog had slipped on the ice and pulled a muscle, but the fever told me something else was happening. I called my veterinarian, who advised special aspirin for the fever. (*Only* give aspirin to your dog on your veterinaran's advice—too much can be toxic.) Two hours later the dog wasn't any better. After consulting with the veterinarian again, we decided the dog needed to be examined.

The diagnosis was meningitis, probably contracted from a small puncture wound in the throat. Meningitis is a fast-moving infection, and if I had ignored the symptoms and waited until the morning, it may have cost my dog his life. Being able to help my veterinarian diagnose the dog's illness by providing the visual observations and temperature readings was important.

Take time each month to look for lumps and sores that may need veterinary attention. Not every lump, bump, and sore needs immediate medical attention, but some malignant tumors can grow very quickly and get out of hand, becoming difficult and expensive to treat. Knowing your dog will enable you to watch for problems. Your dog, just like your kids, will bang into things during playtime, which often results in tenderness or bruising. If the dog bumped into the gate in the yard, you might notice a little swelling at the point of impact. Keep an eye on it, and if it doesn't go down the way a bruise on your own skin would, call the vet.

As dogs age, they develop an array of lumps and bumps, most of the time benign tumors called fatty tumors. Unless one is located on a spot that will irritate the dog in some way, they pose no real problem. You can play it safe by having your veterinarian examine the various lumps and bumps you find when you go in for your dog's checkup, and he can determine which lumps pose a risk to your pet and will advise you to watch them closely for any growth, discharge, or change of texture.

A Canine First Aid Kit

Antibiotic ointment packs   Hydrogen peroxide

Antiseptic cleansing wipes   Insect sting relief pads

Aspirin (low dose)   Kwik Stop

Benadryl   Latex gloves

Burn relief packs   Lubricating jelly pack

Cotton-tipped applicators   Oral syringe (a plastic syringe

Elastic bandage wrap   with the needle removed)

Eye wash   Pepto-Bismol

First aid tape   Scissors

Gauze bandage roll   Thermometer (rectal)

Gauze bandages   Tweezers

If your child and dog collided in the backyard or your dog has any other kind of spill, he may start to limp. It could be a simple tissue injury, which will probably disappear overnight with rest. A cold compress will be soothing and will help the swelling go down. However, if your dog is in very obvious pain, or is still limping and the leg is still swollen the next day, he may have a deep tissue injury, pulled a muscle or ligament, or even broken the leg. It's time to go to the vet.

Watch for unusual bowel movements that contain blood or mucous, and for blood in the urine or urine that is unusually foul smelling or a strange color. All are indications of internal problems. Also look for discharges from the eyes or nose. Watch for unusual discharges from a female in season—a sign of a possible uterine infection. One serious infection is pyometra, which usually occurs about six to eight weeks after a female has been in season, but can happen at other times as well. Signs of this include fever, drinking excessive amounts of water, and discharge from the vagina.

The bottom line is that you need to know what is normal for your dog: appetite, thirst, elimination, sleep, activity level, behavior, body temperature, and physical appearance. When you notice a change in any of these, monitor the situation and do not hesitate to call your veterinarian.

Appropriate Exercise

The only way to maintain your dog in tip-top shape, both physically and mentally, is to give him plenty of exercise. However, you need to be smart about how much and what type of exercise. It is dangerous to take your dog jogging when it is 95 degrees outside. Dogs are cooled through their feet and their mouth, and do not sweat the way we do. Running a dog in the heat builds up the body's temperature and can cause heatstroke. In addition, the pavement may be so hot that his pads may burn or blister. If you must jog on a hot day, try doing it in the early morning or evening when the day and the pavement are cooler.

Think, too, about whether your dog can keep up with you. I often see people jogging or riding a bicycle with their dog lagging behind, tongue hanging out, obviously too small or not in condition to exert that much energy. In planning your exercise routine, ask your dog's breeder and veterinarian for advice.

Before you begin any type of vigorous exercise with your dog, make sure he is in good shape and has no major health problems. Dogs can suffer from heart disease and other problems that will limit their exercise programs. And out of shape or overweight dogs must begin slowly and work up to more vigorous exercise. When exercising any dog, it is important to stop before the dog gets exhausted.

Another consideration in planning your dog's exercise program is his age. Since many breeds suffer from hip and other structural problems, a young dog's exercise program should be limited to twenty to thirty minutes of hard exercise a day, as the repeated impact could stress growing bones and joints. Walking is great exercise for an older dog or a small one (who may have to run to keep pace with your walking), but for a normal healthy dog, it's not enough.

Plain old off-leash running is great for a healthy adult dog. You can do this at dog-approved parks. This enables your dog to stretch his legs, explore, and get fresh air. A good thirty-minute run can really rid him of that pent-up energy while giving you an opportunity to walk and exercise, too. To find a place near you, check with your state's parks or conservation department.

During the warm months, swimming is an excellent form of exercise that dogs of all ages will enjoy. Swimming builds muscle tone and endurance, and aids the cardiovascular system, too. There is no pounding

This Keeshond puppy is cleaning plates his own way.

of the young skeletal frame or joints, so it's fine for puppies. In addition, the cool water keeps your dog from overheating. However, you need to make sure your dog doesn't get too exhausted, as he may tend to enjoy swimming and not know when to quit. Like any exercise, it takes time to build up endurance. It is up to you to recognize when your dog has had enough. It's also important to remember that not every dog knows how to swim—or likes it. Just as you should never let your kids swim alone unsupervised, don't leave your dog alone in the water.

Fencing Your Yard

There are a variety of ways to fence in an area for your dog to play. Fences come in wood, wire (sometimes known as chain-link), and the electric system known as invisible fencing. Whenever possible, I strongly encourage people to install a wooden fence or, for larger areas, wire fencing, which is more affordable.

There are many factors that make traditional wooden or wire fencing a much better choice than an invisible fence. Traditional fences:

- Contain your dog, even if the electricity fails
- Keep other dogs and animals out of your yard, reducing the chances of spreading disease or breeding a female in heat
- Keep children from running through the yard and teasing the dog or getting bitten
- Keep your dog (and your children) safe in areas where coyotes are a problem
- Prevent your dog from chasing squirrels or rabbits, thus keeping him safe from cars
- Reduce the chances your dog will be stolen
- Give you peace of mind when you see the fence

Introducing a New Baby to Your Dog

Are you planning an addition to your family? You'll need to understand, from your dog's point of view, what he thinks is going on. To do that, let's consider what a three-year-old child might be thinking.

We know there is a jealousy phase every child goes through when you bring home a new baby. The older child was used to getting everything when he wanted it, without sharing. Mom's attention was always his, the toys were always his, and the room was always his. Everything in the world was always his.

Now, enter the new baby. All of a sudden mom has additional responsibilities. The newest family member is completely dependent on her for his every need. The older

A Pembroke Welsh Corgi puppy meets the new baby.

child sees that mom's time is not all his anymore. To help in the transition, parents usually try to include the older child in helping to feed, bathe, or change the baby, making the older child "mommy's little helper."

Let's look at this situation again, this time substituting the word "dog" for "child." The dog feels just the same way. In addition, the child grows up and becomes more understanding. The dog stays at the emotional level of a three- to five-year-old child forever.

When you bring the new baby home from the hospital, perhaps grandma and grandpa and some other family members will be waiting at your home. A likely scenario is that you pull into the driveway, grab the bags and the baby, and come into the house. Everyone goes "goo goo" over the baby, the bags are put down, and everyone sits down to admire this bundle of joy. The dog is relegated to the laundry room behind the baby gates, confused and frustrated and having no idea what he did wrong and why he is being separated from this happy occasion. For the dog, who has been a part of the family up until this day, his world is turned inside out. That is when problems develop.

Just as parents prepare an older child for the baby's arrival by letting him touch his mother's tummy and feel the baby kick or helping set up the room or even pick out baby clothes, the dog also needs to be prepared. There are several things you can do. Six weeks before the baby is due, start going in the baby's room from time to time during the day with your dog and let him sniff the crib and tell him he's a good boy. Have a doll in the crib and pick it up, walk around the room with it, and put in back in the crib.

After a few days, introduce a tape of various baby sounds. Once he has become accustomed to the sounds, start opening up packages of baby things, such as powder, lotion, and diapers, for him to sniff.

When the baby is born, take an extra blanket to the hospital and wrap the baby in it for an hour. When dad goes home that night, he should take the blanket home with him and wrap the doll in it. Let the dog sniff, and praise him.

Saba, the Whippet, is much older, but doesn't mind sharing her bed with Andra.

This English Cocker Spaniel is showing by her submissive pose that she is gentle and will not harm the baby.

Now for the big day. The dog is used to the blanket, the smells, and the doll. The most important thing now is that when the family walks in the door, do not ignore the dog. Keep your greeting the same as it was before the baby was born. Let the dog be in the room with you, as part of the family. Carefully let him sniff the baby. He may be a little startled when the baby moves, but continue praising him for his gentleness. Remember not to push too much on him at one time.

Although appropriate preparation will lead to a successful transition, a dog is a dog and small children should never be left alone with any animal without adult supervision. Avoid problems by acting wisely.

8

Career Corner
for Your Child

Often, the experience of growing up with a dog creates a lifetime love of animals. When we were kids and people asked, "What do you want to be when you grow up?" usually only one job came to mind for animal lovers: veterinarian. Today, due to specialization in the veterinary field and the growth of the pet service industry, there are many more opportunities for young people to pursue if they want to work with animals.

There are jobs for veterinary technicians, animal behaviorists, pet food salespeople, kennel operators, doggy daycare workers, dog walkers, pet sitters, professional handlers, wildlife rehabilitation and management workers, zookeepers, professional trainers, groomers, police officers, and military personnel. Let's look at some of these careers more closely.

Veterinarian

To become a Doctor of Veterinary Medicine (DVM) requires four years of graduate school. At this time, so many students want to become vets that it is actually harder to get into veterinary schools than medical schools!

The veterinarians we see are the ones who take care of our pets, but there are also many veterinarians at the forefront of the current war against terrorism, keeping a watchful eye on the nation's food supply and for signs of bioterrorism. They also serve as food inspectors for the U.S. Department of Agriculture and in the military, to make sure proper food sanitation and preparation procedures are followed. Veterinarians also do research at universities, veterinary drug companies, and pet food companies.

A Family of Veterinarians

Dr. Joann Randall and her husband, Dr. Jason Randall, have been veterinarians for twenty-one years. Joann says, "The field is becoming so specialized now. Some doctors work with animals solely with eye disorders, while others work with orthopedic-related problems and others go into research. Even the technicians have areas of expertise."

Before opening their general practice, the Randalls operated an emergency clinic. "Emergency work is fast paced and interesting, it was never dull," Joann says. With specialization growing, many veterinarians no longer do their own after-hours emergency work, and their clients are referred to emergency centers. Now the Randalls are the last general practice veterinarians in their county who offer after-hours emergency services

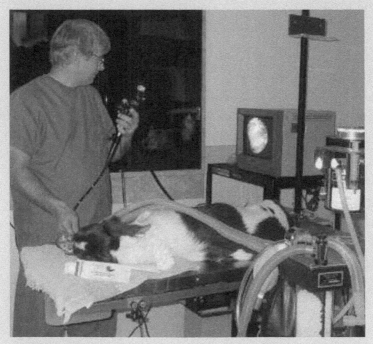

Dr. Jason Randall at the Animal Hospital of Woodstock performing an endoscopic examination of a patient's esophagus and stomach.

for their clients. "It is a service that we provide for our clients because when our assistance is needed, the situation is urgent," Jason says. "Our clients trust us with their animals and we know them best. We have their records and it makes diagnosing ailments much quicker."

The Randalls suggest that anyone interested in becoming a veterinarian get as much animal experience as they can, whether it's working in an animal hospital, on a farm, or training animals. They also say it's important to have good grades throughout school, not just in college. "It all counts," Joann says. They suggest children start with 4-H clubs, if they are available, or at least train their pets and do some competition work, so they can learn about the animals and their care.

Despite the long hours, the Randalls love their work. "It is wonderful to see our patients walk out of the office feeling better than when they came in," Joann says. "We've known many of our clients since they first brought their puppies to us, fourteen years ago. We've developed trust and friendship. Now, in the last few years, hard decisions sometimes have to be made concerning those dogs who are up there in age. It's not easy. Each time we lose one, my husband and I take it personally because we've known them their entire life. I'll retire when losing an animal doesn't bother me anymore. Then I know it's time to quit."

Veterinary Technician

Veterinarians are not the only people who work in veterinary hospitals and clinics. The responsibilities of veterinary technicians can include giving physical examinations, taking patient histories, caring for hospitalized pets, administrating medications and vaccines, performing clinical laboratory procedures, doing dental prophylaxis, taking X-rays, administering anesthesia, and providing surgical assistance.

In addition, they assist in office and medical management and sometimes do research. Becoming a Certified Veterinary Technician (CVT) requires formal academic training and, in the majority of states, veterinary technicians are certified, registered, or licensed. Many veterinary hospitals train vet techs for their own specific needs. These technicians are not certified.

Other career opportunities for trained veterinary technicians include teaching, military service, humane societies, herd health managers, biomedical research, diagnostic laboratories, zoo or wildlife medicine, and veterinary supply sales.

Veterinary Office Manager

Office managers are very important people in a veterinary hospital. They manage the appointment books, handle billing and payments, prepare correspondence and medical records, file, help refer clients to other facilities, order the drugs and supplies, and keep track of work schedules. Secretarial and computer skills are extremely helpful, as is knowledge of medical terminology, good people skills, and the willingness to help out with the animals when necessary.

Wildlife Management

Wildlife managers oversee the stocking of lakes with fish and work as enforcement officers on state and federal land. They manipulate the wild habitat to control the animal population, collect wildlife population figures, and educate the public about conservation. They oversee hunting and fishing. They are concerned with the protection of rare and endangered species.

There are also wildlife researchers and wildlife biologists, who study the physiology, genetics, ecology, behavior, disease, nutrition and population dynamics of animals, and the land usage and pollution patterns of people to see how each affect the animals around us.

The career of a wildlife manager requires serious preparation and long hours of work. Openings in the field are limited, so competition to find a job is stiff. People entering this field must have a strong interest in wildlife, value natural resources, and have a strong science background.

High school students are encouraged to take science, biology, chemistry, physics, math, and computer science to prepare for college.

Children who are interested in a career in wildlife can begin now with activities such as camping, hunting, fishing, bird watching, wildlife photography, and hiking.

Animal Behaviorist

Animal behaviorists study animal behavior and its development, in the wild and in laboratory settings. They seek to understand how external and internal factors affect an animal in its environment and how behavior changes over its lifetime. In addition, they apply behavioral knowledge to the production, management, and conservation of wild and domestic animals. Ethologists are trained in biology, zoology, entomology, wildlife, and other animal sciences. Behaviorists are trained in animal psychology. All types of animal behaviorists usually advance their studies to the graduate level.

Research Assistant

Research assistants usually work at universities, zoos, and museums to help conduct ongoing behavioral research. Working under the direction of faculty and staff, they design and perform tests and then analyze their findings. Research assistants can also be found in zoos and museums, where they usually work in educational programs. The profession requires a love of animals, a meticulous attention to detail, and either a bachelor of science or a master of science degree.

Zoologist

Zoology work is very competitive and demanding, and requires a formal education in animal sciences. Some zookeepers work directly with the animals, while others are responsible for overseeing dietary planning, helping design suitable habitats and activities for the animals, and updating animal records. Zoologists must be able to educate visitors about various species. When special animal exhibits are highlighted, they help to supervise and set up the habitats for the animals' comfort and safety. Suggested classes include biology, chemistry, anatomy, math, English, and speech.

Animal Trainer

Some animal trainers work in the entertainment industry, getting everything from birds to reptiles to cats to perform on camera and in stage work. Although this seems like glamorous work, the hours are long and hard, and the field is very competitive. Often, the best way to get into it is to work for an established animal trainer, learn the ropes, and make as many contacts as possible. A huge love of animals, some training experience, good people skills, and a willingness to work hard are all required.

Far more numerous are the people who make their living as pet dog trainers. Often, dog trainers turn professional after volunteering their services with dog clubs to teach various levels of obedience, conformation, agility, tracking, herding, lure coursing, field trialing, and other disciplines. Trainers may teach private or group lessons. These trainers usually have many years of experience and compete with their dogs. Some trainers have studied animal behavior, but most gain their experience by apprenticing with other professional trainers and handlers in their particular field.

Professional Dog Show Handler

Grace is training her dog for the show ring.

Professional handlers exhibit dogs in conformation shows for their clients. These handlers spend most of the year on the road, taking their clients' dogs from show to show. Between shows, they must keep the dogs groomed, conditioned, exercised, and loved.

There are two routes to becoming a professional handler. The most common is through several years of apprenticeship. The apprentice usually lives with the handler and learns the day-to-day activities of running a kennel, grooming, handling skills, proper conditioning, and the business end of the practice. The second route is by showing your own dogs, scoring many successes, and then setting up shop for others. In this case, you'll need a lot of business sense before you start.

The workday of the professional handler is hard and long, involving exercising dogs, grooming them, and showing them. Weekends are never free: most start with driving to the show, which can be a several-hundred-mile trip. The majority of dog shows require overnight stays. Handlers usually get to their destination the night before to set up their equipment in a place that will be convenient for the entire weekend. This means that multiple crates and exercise pens, grooming equipment, water, and a host of other items need to be unloaded and set up, and dogs fed and exercised for the night.

The hours can be grueling, the travel seemingly endless, but it can be very rewarding if showing dogs is what you love to do.

Professional Field Handler

As with show handlers, a professional field handler's work is highly specialized. Field handlers train dogs to compete in a variety of canine hunting and retrieving activities. The work is done outside in all weather conditions, often on horseback. Many of the big-time field handlers travel via diesel truck, pulling a large trailer unit that also has small living quarters. Their competitive seasons usually coincide with the hunting seasons, in the spring and fall. They may travel on various competition circuits from one end of the country to the other and back again. They are often gone for a good part of the season, which may last three months. During their time off from competition,

This handler is working to steady his dog for competition.

One Handler's Story

Clay Coady began as dog lover, served an apprenticeship with a professional show handler, became well-known himself, and now is a dog show judge.

Coady says his interest in handling dogs was sparked in seventh grade, when he was looking at different careers and realized that what he enjoyed most was competing with his dog. "I trained a Samoyed in conformation, taking him to handling classes, learning to groom and care for him. I entered a show, only to take third place in the Novice Junior Handling class and second in the regular classes. I saw that people were making a living handling and training dogs, and that's when I decided what I wanted to be—a handler. It was fun. Of course, my parents really didn't think my choice was a very good one."

At the age of seventeen, Coady apprenticed with Larry Downey, a well-known and respected handler. "We did a lot of traveling. It was a job that encompassed at least twelve hours a day, seven days a week. Mr. Downey taught me the business side, the conditioning of animals, the health problems, and the psychology of the dogs," Coady recalls.

In 1970, Coady went out on his own. "Showing dogs professionally is very tiring, but it is extremely rewarding when you find the right dog, develop that dog, and take him to the top," he says. As he began to pile up wins, many owners of top dogs wanted him as their professional handler. One of his most well-known clients was Bill Cosby, who shows Lakeland Terriers.

Coady retired from handling in 2001 to pursue a judging career. This means he is still traveling and spends long days on his feet, but it is something he enjoys immensely. In addition, he has opened two large facilities that each house a large kennel, a grooming shop, and a veterinary hospital, and he has plans to expand further.

their job is training dogs for the upcoming season. When the weather is good, they train near home. When the weather turns bad, they usually head for another part of the country.

Clients will often send a dog for training so that the professional can determine whether the dog has the potential to compete. The professional handler can spend eight or more hours in the saddle every day training his clients' dogs. For those handlers who are successful, it is a great way to be their own boss, work outside, and work with animals.

Kennel Owner

Kennels are a big business in this country. People are required to travel for professional and family business more often, and they cannot always take their dog with them or rely on other people for this care in their absence. Kennels vary in size from small (ten to fifteen dogs) to huge (seventy-five to one hundred dogs). Some appeal to the upscale dog owner by providing plush accommodations, radios, and even televisions in the kennel to make their four-legged guests feel more at home. Many facilities also have other services available, such as grooming and training, for their clientele. Owners of these facilities usually employ workers to help feed and exercise the dogs and clean and wash down the kennels. This is a great place for kids to get experience in working with animals.

These facilities must be licensed by the state department of agriculture, meet rigid requirements, and are inspected each year. Appropriate records must be kept for all dogs, including vaccination records and who to call if a dog is sick or injured.

A good business sense, as well as a way with dogs, are required for all kennel owners.

Doggy Daycare Operator

Doggy daycare is similar to a boarding kennel, except the dogs are not housed overnight. It's a social activity for dogs whose owners work all day. Owners drop their dogs off in the morning and pick them up after work.

During the day, the dogs have play periods, training periods, and rest periods, similar to childcare centers. Various services are offered at these facilities, such as obedience training and grooming. This is another way kids can work part time with dogs, since daycare facilities always need to hire people who are good with animals but don't necessarily have formal training.

Dog Walker or Pet Sitter

Many pet owners prefer to have someone come into their home to walk and take care of their pets while they are out working. Services provided by dog walkers can vary, and many also take care of cats, birds, ferrets, and even horses. Some offer to pick up and drop off animals at the groomer's and vet's offices, thereby saving their clients time off from work. A dog walker may be contracted to come in once a day or more to attend to an animal's needs.

Pet sitters look after pets while an owner is traveling. Many also take in the mail, water the plants, and do other small tasks to look after a home. They are the sole caregivers for the pets entrusted to them, and this is a big responsibility.

Dog walkers and pet sitters must be trustworthy, bonded, and insured, because they have all their clients' house keys. They also must be dependable, and must be able to handle dogs and teach them to walk nicely on a leash.

It is important for dog walkers and pet sitters to be very knowledgeable about health considerations in animals. One of the responsibilities they often take on is administering medications to animals. And if a pet becomes ill while the owner is away, the pet sitter must act immediately. Knowing how to take temperatures, check for shock, and respond in emergencies is vital. Recognizing an ailment that is relatively minor as opposed to a serious illness or injury is also very important.

Pet sitting can be an excellent job for a responsible teenager over the summer and vacation breaks, but it requires a serious commitment. Not one single visit for one single animal can be skipped. If your child is not feeling well one day, someone else must take over.

Pet Food and Veterinary Supply Sales

People who enjoy animals and sales work often find this type of job very rewarding. They usually travel within a specific area to various pet shops, kennels, and veterinarians to talk about their products. In addition, they may attend animal events and shows, promoting the products as exhibitors. Salespeople are very knowledgeable about the things they sell and the products of their competitors. These people need a good understanding of animal nutrition and health. Bachelor's degrees in marketing and computer classes are extremely helpful.

Groomer

Becoming a groomer can give a person an opportunity to be their own boss, have their own shop, and make their own decisions, all while doing something they love. A professional groomer needs formal training in the styling procedures of the different dog breeds, and there are trade schools that teach this. Students learn styling and cutting, anatomy, proper grooming techniques for different types of coat, basic health concerns a groomer might come across, and techniques for handling dogs. Many times, it is the groomer who finds a health problem, such as an injury or a growth, while working on a dog.

Groomers find work in many places. In addition to owning their own shop, groomers are employed in veterinary clinics and pet supply stores. One groomer I know bought a truck that she uses as her shop and drives from one appointment to another every day.

Photographer

There are wildlife photographers who help researchers capture the behavior and beauty of animals, work on documentaries, and give scientists and the public glimpses of

Donna Witkowski does the final touch-up before a show for this Golden Retriever, owned by Larry Larsen.

the animal world. Other photographers specialize in pet photography. Still other photographers make their living at dog shows and sporting events, catching the thrill of victory. For someone interested in pursuing this as a career, formal training in photography and art is required. Other photographers find a niche providing pictures for magazines and newspapers or specialized calendars, or offering personalized services for clients who are looking for special photos.

Law Enforcement and Search and Rescue

September 11, 2001, focused a great deal of attention on the important work military, law enforcement, and search and rescue dogs do around the world. Today, dogs in K-9 corps are used at airports, schools, government buildings, and other venues that require heightened security. They are trained to detect explosives and drugs. They are used by police agencies for search and rescue, cadaver work, crowd control, and tracking, and in situations that may be too dangerous for humans.

Search and rescue dogs find people who are lost as well as those who are being pursued by law enforcement. Mark Graf, a K-9 officer for a town in the northern suburbs of Chicago, says one of his best moments as a police officer was on such as rescue mission. "A call came in about a missing elderly man. My K-9 partner, a German Shepherd named Alf, and I tracked his scent. We found him scared but safe in some bushes. There is a great satisfaction in helping someone get back with their loved ones safe and sound." Graf and Alf have also helped find a lost child as well as apprehend criminals and drug dealers.

Cadaver dogs are specifically trained to find accident, disaster, and murder victims. Since evidence is crucial in convicting criminals, the work these dogs perform have solved many police cases and given closure to many victims' families.

Working as a K-9 officer requires a great deal of dedication. Dog handlers may be called to work on a case even when they are not on duty. Many off-duty hours are taken up with ongoing dog training in tracking, search or protection work, or drugs or explosives detection. Every officer and their K-9 companion must be in top physical condition.

Most police departments recruit K-9 officers from within their own ranks, and not all departments and agencies have K-9 units. Many programs require at least two years of experience as a police officer. In selecting officers to work in the K-9 unit, the first consideration is a love of dogs. Experience with dog handling and training is considered a big plus. People interested in this vocation often major in criminal justice in college. Applicants must also have a flexible family situation, because when an emergency arises and a dog and handler team is needed, they must go. Hours are long, and handlers need to be able to make snap decisions that could include the safety of both themselves and their dog.

Two excellent Web sites that offer a wealth of information are www. leerburg.com and www.uspcak9.com.

These are just a few of the careers with animals your child might be interested in. There are many more animal-related opportunities in marine science, research organizations, shelters, and pet supply stores. To investigate all the possibilities, contact a career counselor at your child's school or your local community college.

Officer Pat Behles and her partner, Keesha (Rena Vom Sturm und Drang VCD1, CD, TD, TC, OA, AXJ, CGC, TDI, U-CD, OAC, OGC, OJC).

Appendix A

Registries and the Breeds They Recognize

The three largest registries in North America are the American Kennel Club, the Canadian Kennel Club, and the United Kennel Club. (There are also smaller registries, such as the States Kennel Club, and the International Kennel Club.) Each keeps track of breeding records, ownership records, and title records earned by dogs registered under their domain. Each also makes rules regarding the canine sports it sanctions and approves judges for those sports.

American Kennel Club

5580 Centerview Drive
Suite 200
Raleigh, NC 27606-3390
(919) 233-9767
www.akc.org

The American Kennel Club (AKC) was formed in 1884 when dog fanciers and breeders felt a need for a reliable way of recording pedigrees. The club built its original studbook records from three volumes of donated books from East Coast fanciers and held shows modeled after the ones in Great Britain. The AKC has no individual members, but has many member clubs.

There are currently 156 breeds and varieties that are fully recognized by the AKC, plus three more in the Miscellaneous Class; more breeds are added as they meet the requirements for AKC recognition. The recognized breeds when this book was written are:

Sporting Group

American Water Spaniel

Brittany

Chesapeake Bay Retriever

Clumber Spaniel

Cocker Spaniel

Curly-Coated Retriever

English Cocker Spaniel

English Setter

English Springer Spaniel

Field Spaniel

Flat-Coated Retriever

German Shorthaired Pointer

German Wirehaired Pointer

Golden Retriever

Gordon Setter

Irish Setter

Irish Water Spaniel

Labrador Retriever

Nova Scotia Duck Tolling
    Retriever

Pointer

Spinone Italiano

Sussex Spaniel

Vizsla

Weimaraner

Welsh Springer Spaniel

Wirehaired Pointing Griffon

Hound Group

Afghan Hound

Basenji

Basset Hound

Beagle

Black and Tan Coonhound

Bloodhound

Borzoi

Dachshund

Foxhound, American

Foxhound, English

Greyhound

Harrier

Ibizan Hound

Irish Wolfhound

Norwegian Elkhound

Otterhound

Petit Basset Griffon Vendéen

Pharaoh Hound

Rhodesian Ridgeback

Saluki

Scottish Deerhound

Whippet

Working Group

Akita

Alaskan Malamute

Anatolian Shepherd

Bernese Mountain Dog

Black Russian Terrier

Boxer

Bullmastiff

Doberman Pinscher

German Pinscher

Giant Schnauzer

Great Dane

Great Pyrenees

Greater Swiss Mountain Dog

Komondor

Kuvasz

Mastiff

Neapolitan Mastiff

Newfoundland

Portuguese Water Dog

Rottweiler

St. Bernard

Samoyed

Siberian Husky

Standard Schnauzer

Terrier Group

Airedale Terrier

American Staffordshire Terrier

Australian Terrier

Bedlington Terrier

Border Terrier

Bull Terrier

Cairn Terrier

Dandie Dinmont Terrier

Glen of Imaal Terrier

Irish Terrier

Kerry Blue Terrier

Lakeland Terrier

Miniature Bull Terrier

Miniature Schnauzer

Norfolk Terrier

Norwich Terrier

Parson Russell Terrier

Scottish Terrier

Sealyham Terrier

Skye Terrier

Smooth Fox Terrier

Soft Coated Wheaten Terrier

Staffordshire Bull Terrier

Standard Manchester Terrier

Welsh Terrier

West Highland White Terrier

Wire Fox Terrier

Toy Group

Affenpinscher

Brussels Griffon

Cavalier King Charles Spaniel

Chihuahua

Chinese Crested

English Toy Spaniel

Havanese

Italian Greyhound

Japanese Chin

Maltese

Miniature Pinscher

Papillon

Pekingese

Pomeranian

Pug

Shih Tzu

Silky Terrier

Toy Fox Terrier

Toy Manchester Terrier

Toy Poodle

Yorkshire Terrier

Non-Sporting Group

American Eskimo Dog	Keeshond
Bichon Frise	Lhasa Apso
Boston Terrier	Löwchen
Bulldog	Miniature Poodle
Chinese Shar-Pei	Schipperke
Chow Chow	Shiba Inu
Dalmatian	Standard Poodle
Finnish Spitz	Tibetan Spaniel
French Bulldog	Tibetan Terrier

Herding Group

Australian Cattle Dog	Canaan Dog
Australian Shepherd	Cardigan Welsh Corgi
Bearded Collie	Collie
Belgian Malinois	German Shepherd Dog
Belgian Sheepdog	Old English Sheepdog
Belgian Tervuren	Pembroke Welsh Corgi
Border Collie	Polish Lowland Sheepdog
Bouvier des Flandres	Puli
Briard	Shetland Sheepdog

Miscellaneous Class

Beauceron	Redbone Coonhound
Plott Hound	

AKC Foundation Stock Service

5580 Centerview Drive
Suite 200
Raleigh, NC 27606-3390
(919) 233-9767
www.akc.org

The Foundation Stock Service (FSS) was created by the American
Kennel Club so that fanciers of breeds not recognized by the AKC
would have a reliable registry to keep their records. The breeds that are
currently registered by the FSS are:

American English Coonhound	Cesky Terrier
Appenzeller Mountain Dog	Chinook
Argentine Dogo	Coton de Tulear
Azawakh	Czechoslovakian Wolfdog
Beauceron	Dogue de Bordeaux
Belgian Laekenois	Entlebucher Mountain Dog
Bergamasco	Estrela Mountain Dog
Black and Tan Coonhound*	Finnish Lapphund
Bluetick Coonhound	German Spitz
Bolognese	Grand Bassett Griffon Vendeen
Boykin Spaniel	Icelandic Sheepdog
Bracco Italiano	Irish Red and White Setter
Cane Corso	Kai Ken
Catahoula Leopard Dog	Koolkerhondje
Caucasian Mountain Dog	Lagotto Romagnolo
Central Asian Shepherd Dog	Lancashire Heeler

* The FSS keeps the registry of the Black and Tan Coonhound Club, which is a hunting
dog registry that does not plan on seeking AKC recognition. Their dogs are from different
bloodlines than the AKC-recognized Black and Tan Coonhound.

Leonberger	Redbone Coonhound
Mudi	Sloughi
Norwegian Buhund	Swedish Vallhund
Norwegian Lundehund	Thai Ridgeback
Perro de Presa Canario	Tibetan Mastiff
Peruvian Inca Orchid	Tosa
Portugese Podengo	Treeing Tennessee Brindle
Pumi	Treeing Walker Coonhound
Pyrenean Shepherd	Xoloitzcuintli
Rat Terrier	

United Kennel Club

United Kennel Club, Inc.
100 E. Kilgore Road
Kalamazoo, MI 49002-5584.
(269) 343-9020
www.ukcdogs.com

The United Kennel Club (UKC) is the second oldest registry in the United States. It was founded in 1898. Its founder, Chauncey Bennett, wanted his registry to emphasize working dogs doing what they were bred to do. This registry was the first to use DNA profiling as a method of identification and proof of parentage. DNA profiling assists in maintaining an accurate stud registry for the breed.

The UKC recognizes 306 breeds, twice the number of the AKC. They are:

Companion Breeds

Affenpinscher	Boston Terrier
Bichon Frise	Brussels Griffon
Bolognese	Cavalier King Charles Spaniel

Chihuahua

Chinese Crested

Coton de Tulear

Dalmatian

English Bulldog

English Toy Spaniel

French Bulldog

Havanese

Italian Greyhound

Japanese Chin

Lhasa Apso

Löwchen

Maltese

Miniature Pinscher

Papillon

Pekingese

Peruvian Inca Orchid

Pomeranian

Poodle (Miniature and Toy)

Pug

Schipperke

Shih Tzu

Tibetan Spaniel

Tibetan Terrier

Yorkshire Terrier

Guardian Dogs

Akbash Dog

American Bulldog

Anatolian Shepherd

Appenzeller

Bernese Mountain Dog

Black Russian Terrier

Boxer

Bull Mastiff

Caucasian Ovtcharka

Central Asian Shepherd Dog

Danish Broholmer

Doberman Pinscher

Dogo Argentino

Dogue de Bordeaux

Entlebucher

Estrela Mountain Dog

Great Dane

Great Pyrenees

Greater Swiss Mountain Dog

Hovawart

Kangal Dog

Komondor

Krasky Ovcar

Kuvasz

Leonberger

Maremma Sheepdog

Mastiff

Neapolitan Mastiff

Newfoundland

Owczarek Podhalanski

Perro de Presa Canario

Rottweiler

St. Bernard

Sarplaninac

Slovac Cuvac

South Russian Ovcharka

Spanish Mastiff

Tibetan Mastiff

Tosa Ken

Gun Dogs

American Water Spaniel

Barbet

Boykin Spaniel

Bracco Italiano

Braque D'Auvergne

Braque du Bourbonnais

Braque Francais, de Grande Taille

Braque Francais, de Petite Taille

Braque Saint-Germain

Brittany Spaniel

Cesky Fousek

Chesapeake Bay Retriever

Clumber Spaniel

Cocker Spaniel

Curly-Coated Retriever

Deutscher Wachtelhund (German Spaniel)

Drentse Patrijshond

English Cocker Spaniel

English Pointer

English Setter

English Springer Spaniel

Epagneul Blue de Picardie

Epagneul Breton

Epagneul Picard

Epagneul Pont-Audemer

Appendix A

Field Spaniel

Flat-Coated Retriever

French Spaniel (Epagneul
   Francais)

German Longhaired Pointer

German Shorthaired Pointer

German Wirehaired Pointer

Golden Retriever

Gordon Setter

Irish Red and White Setter

Irish Setter

Irish Water Spaniel

Kooikerhondje

Labrador Retriever

Large Munsterlander

Nova Scotia Duck Tolling
   Retriever

Old Danish Bird Dog

Perdiguero de Burgos

Perdiguero Navarro

Portuguese Pointer (Perdiguero
   Portugueso)

Pudelpointer

Small Munsterlander

Spanish Water Dog

Spinone Italiano

Stabyhoun

Standard Poodle

Sussex Spaniel

Vizsla

Weimaraner

Welsh Springer Spaniel

Wirehaired Pointing Griffon

Herding Dogs

Australian Cattle Dog

Australian Kelpie

Australian Shepherd

Bearded Collie

Beauceron

Belgian Shepherd Dog
   (Groenendael, Laekenois,
   Malinois, Tervuren)

Bergamasco

Berger de Pyrenees

Berger Picard (Picardy Shepherd)

Border Collie

Bouvier des Flandres

Briard

Collie

Dutch Shepherd

English Shepherd

German Shepherd Dog

Giant Schnauzer

Louisiana Catahoula Leopard Dog

Mudi

Old English Sheep Dog

Polski Owczarek Nizinny

Puli

Pumi

Schapendoes

Shetland Sheepdog

Standard Schnauzer

Stumpy Tail Cattle Dog

Swedish Vallhund

Welsh Corgi-Cardigan

Welsh Corgi-Pembroke

White Shepherd

Northern Breeds

Ainu

Akita

Alaskan Klee Kai

Alaskan Malamute

American Eskimo

Canadian Eskimo Dog

Chinese Shar-Pei

Chinook

Chow Chow

East Siberian Laika

Eurasian

Finnish Lapphund

Finnish Spitz

Greenland Dog

Iceland Dog

Jindo

Kai

Karelian Bear Dog

Keeshond

Lundehund

Norbottenspets

Norwegian Buhund

Norwegian Elkhound

Russo-European Laika

Samoyed

Shiba

Siberian Husky

Swedish Lapphund

West Siberian Laika

Scent Hounds

Alpine Dachsbracke

American Black and Tan
  Coonhound

American Foxhound

Anglo-Francais de Moyen Venerie

Anglo-Francais de Petit Venerie

Ariegeois

Basset Artesien Normand

Basset Bleu de Gascogne

Basset Fauve De Bretagne

Basset Hound

Bavarian Mountain Hound

Beagle

Beagle Harrier

Billy

Black Forest Hound

Black Mouth Cur

Bloodhound

Bluetick Coonhound

Briquette Griffon Vendeen

Chien D'Artois

Chien Francais Blanc et Noir

Chien Francais Black et Orange

Chien Francais Tricolore

Dachshund

Deutsche Bracke

Drever

Dunker

English Coonhound

English Foxhound

Estonian Hound

Finnish Hound

Grand Anglo-Francais

Grand Basset Griffon Vendeen

Grand Bleu de Gascogne

Grand Gascon-Saintongeois

Grand Griffon Vendeen

Griffon Fauve de Bretagne

Griffon Nivernais

Hamiltonstovare

Hanoverian Hound

Harrier

Large Spanish Hound (Sabueso
  Español de Monte)

Leopard Cur

Mountain Cur

Otterhound

Petit Basset Griffon Vendeen

Petit Bleu de Gascogne

Petit Gascon-Saintongeois

Petit Griffon Bleu de Gascogne

Plott Hound

Poitevin

Polish Hound

Porcelaine

Redbone Coonhound

Small Spanish Hound (Sabueso Español Lebero)

Stephens' Cur

Treeing Cur

Treeing Walker Coonhound

Welsh Hound

Sight Hounds and Pariah Dogs

Afghan Hound

Azawakh

Basenji

Borzoi

Canaan Dog

Carolina Dog

Chart Polski

Greyhound

Ibizan Hound

Irish Wolfhound

New Guinea Singing Dog

Pharaoh Hound

Podengo Portugueso

Rhodesian Ridgeback

Saluki

Scottish Deerhound

Sloughi

Spanish Greyhound

Thai Ridgeback

Whippet

Xoloitzcuintli

Terriers

Airedale Terrier

American Hairless Terrier

American Pit Bull Terrier

Australian Terrier

Bedlington Terriers

Border Terrier

Bull Terrier

Cairn Terrier

Cesky Terrier

Dandie Dinmont Terrier

German Pinscher

Glen of Imaal Terrier

Irish Terrier

Jack Russell Terrier

Jagdterrier

Kerry Blue Terrier

Kromfohrlander

Lakeland Terrier

Manchester Terrier

Miniature Bull Terrier

Miniature Schnauzer

Norfolk Terrier

Norwich Terrier

Patterdale Terrier

Rat Terrier

Russell Terrier

Scottish Terrier

Sealyham Terrier

Silky Terrier

Skye Terrier

Smooth Fox Terrier

Soft-Coated Wheaten Terrier

Sporting Lucas Terrier

Staffordshire Bull Terrier

Teddy Roosevelt Terrier

Toy Fox Terrier

Treeing Feist

Welsh Terrier

West Highland White Terrier

Wire Fox Terrier

Appendix B

Web Sites of the National Breed Clubs

These Web sites will open doors in your research efforts. The sites listed here are for the national breed club for each breed recognized by the American Kennel Club (AKC). You will find information on health, breed rescue contacts, a frequently asked questions section (which is a must to look at), and links to breed information, national and local club listings and contacts, health surveys, pictures, descriptions, upcoming events—you name it and it's there. So open that door and investigate!

Affenpinscher Club of America, www.affenpinscher.org

Afghan Hound Club of America, clubs.akc.org/ahca

Airedale Terrier Club of America, www.airedale.org

Akita Club of America, www.akitaclub.org

Alaskan Malamute Club of America, www.alaskanmalamute.org

American [Cocker] Spaniel Club, www.asc-cockerspaniel.org

American Eskimo Dog Club of America, mywebpages.comcast.net/jamarsch/aedca/index.html

Staffordshire Terrier Club of America, www.amstaff.org

American Water Spaniel Club, www.americanwaterspanielclub.org

Anatolian Shepherd Dog Club of America, www.asdca.org

Australian Cattle Dog Club of America, www.acdca.org

United States Australian Shepherd Association, www.australianshepherds. org

Australian Terrier Club of America, www.australianterrier.org

Basenji Club of America, www.basenji.org

Basset Hound Club of America, www.basset-bhca.org

National Beagle Club, clubs.akc.org/NBC/index.html

Bearded Collie Club of America, www.beardie.net/bcca

North American Beauceron Club, www.beauce.org

Bedlington Terrier Club of America, clubs.akc.org/btca

American Belgian Malinois Club, www.breedclub.org/ABMC.htm

Belgian Sheepdog Club of America, www.bsca.info

American Belgian Tervuren Club, www.abtc.org

Bernese Mountain Dog Club of America, www.bmdca.org

Bichon Frise Club of America, www.bichon.org

Black Russian Terrier Club of America, www.brtca.org

American Black and Tan Coonhound Club, www.abtcc.com

American Bloodhound Club, www.bloodhounds.org

Border Collie Society of America, www.bordercolliesociety.com

Border Terrier Club of America, clubs.akc.org/btcoa

Borzoi Club of America, www.borzoiclubofamerica.org

Boston Terrier Club of America, www.bostonterrierclubofamerica.org/

American Bouvier des Flandres Club, www.bouvier.org

American Boxer Club, americanboxerclub.org/

Briard Club of America, www.briardclubofamerica.org/

American Brittany Club, clubs.akc.org/brit

American Brussels Griffon Association, www.brussels-griffon.info/

Bulldog Club of America, www.thebca.org

American Bullmastiff Association, clubs.akc.org/aba/index.html

Bull Terrier Club of America, www.btca.com

Cairn Terrier Club of America, www.cairnterrier.org

Canaan Dog Club of America, www.cdca.org

Cardigan Welsh Corgi Club of America, www.cardigancorgis.com

American Cavalier King Charles Spaniel Club, www.ackcsc.org

American Chesapeake Club, www.amchessieclub.org

Chihuahua Club of America, www.chihuahuaclubofamerica.com

American Chinese Crested Club, www.crestedclub.org

Chinese Shar-Pei Club of America, www.cspca.com

Chow Chow Club, www.chowclub.org

Clumber Spaniel Club of America, www.clumbers.org

Collie Club of America, www.collieclubofamerica.org

Curly-Coated Retriever Club of America, www.ccrca.org

Dachshund Club of America, www.dachshund-dca.org

Dalmatian Club of America, www.thedca.org

Dandie Dinmont Terrier Club of America, clubs.akc.org/ddtca/index.html

Doberman Pinscher Club of America, www.dpca.org

English Cocker Spaniel Club of America, www.ecsca.org

English Setter Association of America, www.esaa.com

English Springer Spaniel Field Trial Association, www.essfta.org

English Toy Spaniel Club of America, www.etsca.org

Field Spaniel Society of America, clubs.akc.org/fssa/

Finnish Spitz Club of America, www.finnishspitzclub.org

Flat-Coated Retriever Society of America, www.fcrsainc.org

American Fox Terrier Club, www.aftc.org

American Foxhound Club, Inc, www.americanfoxhoundclubinc.com

English Foxhound Club of America, see www.akc.org

French Bulldog Club of America, www.frenchbulldogclub.org

German Pinscher Club of America, www.german-pinscher.com

German Shepherd Dog Club of America, www.gsdca.org

German Shorthaired Pointer Club of America, www.gspca.org

German Wirehaired Pointer Club of America, www.gwpca.com

Giant Schnauzer Club of America, clubs.akc.org/gsca/

Glen of Imaal Terrier Club of America, www.glens.org

Golden Retriever Club of America, www.grca.org

Gordon Setter Club of America, www.gsca.org

Great Dane Club of America, www.gdca.org

Great Pyrenees Club of America, clubs.akc.org/gpca/

Greater Swiss Mountain Dog Club of America, www.gsmdca.org

Greyhound Club of America, www.greyhoundclubofamerica.org

Harrier Club of America, www.ridgecrest.ca.us/~auborn/harriers/HCA.html

Havanese Club of America, www.havanese.org

Ibizan Hound Club of the United States, www.geocities.com/Heartland/
  Pointe/2446/IHCUS.htm

Irish Setter Club of America, www.irishsetterclub.org

Irish Terrier Club of America, www.dogbiz.com/itca/

Irish Water Spaniel Club of America, clubs.akc.org/iwsc/

Irish Wolfhound Club of America, www.iwclubofamerica.org

Italian Greyhound Club of America, www.italiangreyhound.org

Japanese Chin Club of America, www.japanesechin.org

Keeshond Club of America, www.keeshond.org

United States Kerry Blue Terrier Club, www.uskbtc.com

Komondor Club of America, clubs.akc.org/kca/

Kuvasz Club of America, www.kuvasz.com

Labrador Retriever Club, www.thelabradorclub.com

United States Lakeland Terrier Club, clubs.akc.org/usltc/index.htm

American Lhasa Apso Club, www.lhasaapso.org

Löwchen Club of America, madriglace2@yahoo.com

American Maltese Association, www.americanmaltese.org

American Manchester Terrier Club, clubs.akc.org/mtca/index.htm

Mastiff Club of America, www.mastiff.org

Miniature Bull Terrier Club of America, www.mbtca.org

Miniature Pinscher Club of America, www.minpin.org

American Miniature Schnauzer Club, www.amsc.us

United States Neapolitan Mastiff Club, www.neapolitan.org

Newfoundland Club of America, www.newfdogclub.org

Norwegian Elkhound Association of America, www.neaa.net

Norwich and Norfolk Terrier Club, clubs.akc.org/nntc/

Nova Scotia Duck Tolling Retriever Club (USA), www.nsdtrc-usa.org

Old English Sheepdog Club of America, clubs.akc.org/oesca

Otterhound Club of America, clubs.akc.org/ohca/

Papillon Club of America, www.papillonclub.org

Parson Russell Terrier Association of America, www.jrtaa.org

Pekingese Club of America, www.geocities.com/Heartland/3843

Pembroke Welsh Corgi Club of America, www.pembrokecorgi.org

Petit Basset Griffon Vendeen Club of America, www.pbgv.org

Pharaoh Hound Club of America, www.pharaohhca.com

American Plott Hound Association, american-plott.assn.@usa.net

American Pointer Club, www.americanpointerclub.org

American Polish Lowland Sheepdog Club, www.aponc.com

American Pomeranian Club, www.americanpomeranianclub.org

Poodle Club of America, www.poodleclubofamerica.org

Portuguese Water Dog Club of America, www.pwdca.org

Pug Dog Club of America, www.pugs.org

Puli Club of America, www.puliclub.org

Redbone Treehound Association, see www.akc.org

Rhodesian Ridgeback Club of the United States, www.rrcus.org

American Rottweiler Club, www.amrottclub.org

Saluki Club of America, www.salukiclub.org

Samoyed Club of America, www.samoyed.org/Samoyed_Club_of_
America.html

Schipperke Club of America, www.schipperkeclub-usa.org/

Scottish Deerhound Club of America, www.deerhound.org

Scottish Terrier Club of America, clubs.akc.org/stca

American Sealyham Terrier Club, clubs.akc.org/sealy

American Shetland Sheepdog Association, www.assa.org

National Shiba Club of America, www.shibas.org/index.html

American Shih Tzu Club, www.shihtzu.org

Siberian Husky Club of America, www.shca.org

Silky Terrier Club of America, silkyterrierclubofamerica.org

Skye Terrier Club of America, clubs.akc.org/skye

Soft Coated Wheaten Terrier Club of America, www.scwtca.org

Spinone Club of America, www.spinone.com

St. Bernard Club of America, www.saintbernardclub.org

Staffordshire Bull Terrier Club, www.clubs.akc.org/sbtci

Standard Schnauzer Club of America, www.geocities.com/Yosemite/7068

Sussex Spaniel Club of America, www.sussexspaniels.org

Tibetan Spaniel Club of America, www.tsca.ws

Tibetan Terrier Club of America, www.ttca-online.org

American Toy Fox Terrier Club, www.atftc.com

Vizsla Club of America, clubs.akc.org/vizsla

Weimaraner Club of America, www.weimclubamerica.org

Welsh Springer Spaniel Club of America, www.wssca.com

Welsh Terrier Club of America, clubs.akc.org/wtca

West Highland White Terrier Club of America, www.westieclubamerica.com

American Whippet Club, www.americanwhippetclub.net

American Wirehaired Pointing Griffon Association, www.awpga.com

Yorkshire Terrier Club of America, www.ytca.org

Picture Credits

Photo pp. 3, 11, 25, 31, 57, 83, 115, 137, Robin Schwartz; pp. 6, 62, Lesley Forman; pp. 8, 17, Cathy Gallagher, Sienna Pointe Vizslas; p. 10, Janice July; p. 16, Patti Runchey; p. 18, Marge Mehagian, Mehagian Vizslas; p. 23, Vicki Waciega; p. 29, Michael Shupp; p. 34, Karin Boullion, Gold Boullion Golden Retrievers; p. 35, Carol Carchietta; pp. 20, 38, 85, 111, 121, Sharon Sakson; p. 45, Diana Stromley; p. 68, Brad Wood; p. 71, Barry Levitt; p. 73, Amy Kluth; p. 78, Tim Dyer; p. 87, John Mehagian; p. 95, Karen L. Stromley; p. 99, Garden Studio Inc.; pp. 103, 108, 147, 149, Cheryl Peterson, Nordic Versatile Vizslas; p. 104, Animal Hospital of Woodstock; p. 107, Jane Cooney Waterhouse; p. 112, Pet Personalities, Photo by Alissa Behr; p. 132, Heather Myers; p. 133, Paula Caffee; p. 134, Drew Sakson; p. 142, Donna Bennett.

Index

About the Author

I have been involved in the sport of dogs since 1972, when my family purchased a Weimaraner from a well-known breeder in central Illinois. In 1973, my family became interested in showing and training dogs under the guidance of Russell Harmon, the owner of our puppy's sire. I helped to finish the conformation championship on our first dog, Ch. Bubchen's Liebchen v. Kleefeld, NSD, NRD, SD, RD, SDX, CD, VX, with the help of Carl and Martha Amweg, PHA, and Russ. Hooked on the sport, my family branched out into other areas of competition, such as field work, agility, and obedience.

As a result, under the kennel name Nordic, my family has owned and/or bred many champions and dogs with titles in field, agility, and obedience, as well as dogs ranked in the Top Ten of conformation and agility and Top Producers.

In 1980, I decided to pursue my interests professionally in the show ring and have had the honor of handling several top-ranked field Vizslas in the conformation ring, as well as Weimaraners and many other breeds.

In my spare time, I teach obedience and conformation classes for local kennel clubs and have consulted with families searching for dogs. I have also stayed in touch with many families to help them find training programs for their dogs.

Judging was the next step for me, and I obtained my AKC approval as a judge for Hunt Tests and Field Trials. Currently, I am working on gaining approval for AKC conformation judging.

Along with my mother, Bette Peterson, I have been involved in rescue work for more than twenty years, and it is this work that prompted me to write this book.

I am affiliated with the Weimaraner Club of America, Inc., the Weimaraner Club of Northern Illinois, Inc., the Vizsla Club of America, Inc., the Vizsla Club of Illinois, Inc., the Glenbard All-Breed Obedience

Club, Inc., and the Northwest Obedience Club, Inc., and have held many active positions with these clubs.

I have bred and/or owned fifteen stellar and multititled Weimaraners (including several rescue dogs) and five outstanding and multititled Vizslas. Two of our top-winning Weimaraners include Ch. Nordicstar-N Milkyway, bred and owned by us, who was the number-one Weimaraner bitch in conformation in 1979. Her sister, Ch. Nordicstar-N Sagitta, won the 1978 Eastern Bench Futurity, the largest futurity winner in breed history, a record that still stands today. On the Vizsla front, we own UACHX Ch. Mehagian's Zip-A-Dee-Doo-Dah, SH, CD, OA, OAP, AXP, OAJ, OJP, CGC, VC. Zippy is truly a versatile dog, earning twenty-three titles in four areas of competition.